Come On Along

Also by Ben Mukkala

Tour Guide: Big Bay and Huron Mountains

Copper, Timber, Iron and Heart

Come On Along

by

Ben Mukkala

Third Printing

Still Waters Publishing
Marquette   Michigan
2002

Come On Along

All photography in this book is the work of the author unless
indicated otherwise.

Published by Still Waters Publishing, 2002

Third Edition • 1,000 copies • September 2004

ISBN   0-9709971-1-6

In Nature there are no laws,

there are only consequences.

Dedication

"... The purpose of life is to *matter* – to count, to stand for something, to have it make some difference that we have lived at all."

Leo C. Rosten

This book is respectfully dedicated to

You,

The Reader

If these pages bring you enjoyment, if they give a little insight, if they make your burdens a little lighter, then I have "made some difference," I have "mattered."

Acknowledgements

This page is to acknowledge the help received from others. It recognizes those you couldn't have done without and is a plea for forgiveness from those you have disappointed. I don't know that it interests a reader but it fulfills an obligation to confess shortcomings.

I should have to include all those who taught me about life and living, the outdoors, the standards and ethics by which I believe a "good" person should abide. A fella's mother and father immediately come to mind but there were many others. I should also include the creatures of the natural world, fish, fur and fowl - even mosquitoes - it has been my privilege to observe, to know, and to learn from. And there were a couple of wars. There's nothing like a war to tear the meaningless tinsel from the fundamentals of life.

For the immediate task I must thank my wife, Dorothy, for her never failing encouragement and assistance. Responsibility for any and all mistakes of course is mine.

Last but far from least, I wish to thank you, the reader, for taking the time to consider my efforts. I sincerely hope I don't disappoint you.

Ω

Table of Contents

♎

Index of photographs

Ω

Come On Along

Foreword

The purpose of this book is entertainment – your entertainment. It is directed at those who enjoy the outdoors, life, and living. I was an avid hunter during my younger years. I still enjoy the woods, the creatures that live there, fishing (mostly catch-and-release) and the camaraderie and companionship of "Deer Camp." I no longer have the urge to kill anything. I'll eat it – I just don't want to kill it. Go figure.

Today's hunting seems more business than sport. Inviting a creature to dine with you then shooting it as it sits down to eat - well - something's wrong there. The title "Hunter" suggests searching, planning, and exhibiting some skill and ability as a woodsman. The killing is aftermath. To me, "it's not the gold that I'm wanting so much as just finding the gold." Over the years I have found "gold." Let me tell you about it. Maybe you'll find a little gold yourself.

Since some of these stories have been published in magazines and newspapers some incidental repetition occurs. I ask your tolerance.

"Any resemblance in these writings to actual people, living or dead, is purely coincidental." Some of you may see a resemblance to people you know or knew - and it's all right - just don't tell anyone.

Ω

Come On Along

The Animals

Humans are inclined to look upon animals as lesser beings. We view them as below us, without emotions or feelings. We kill these creatures and eat them. Almost all of us utilize meat or meat related products every day. Relegating them to a subservient status, categorizing them, as "beasts of the field" seems to makes these actions acceptable.

I am not a vegetarian nor do I intend to become one. I accept the fact that animals live in a separate world and serve the needs of humans. I also recognize that in many ways they are superior to me. They hear things I can't hear. Some have sight far superior to mine. Many have a sense of smell that far exceeds any human's. They live beside us but in a different world. Their mental capacity and physical abilities are uniquely adapted to the world in which they survive.

The Indians too, relied on the creatures of the forest for food, clothing and shelter. They however treated the animal with great respect. Whenever they killed one they held a ceremony of appreciation and thanksgiving. They thanked the animal's spirit for sacrificing life that the Indian might live.

These living things of woods, wind, and water are not lower beings. We hunt them, kill them, eat them but we should also respect them. They are separate beings existing with us in this one world in which we all live.

♎

Come On Along

Barred Owl

**A barred owl gazes down at this intruder in its domain. With
its acute hearing there's not much danger of something
approaching undetected.**

The Barred Owl

I built a nesting box for a barred owl. The
directions and dimensions were in the back of some
outdoor magazine. It seems a little strange that a
bird who has been living for years in knot holes and
hollow dead trees suddenly has an architect but a
person has got to start somewhere. I'd heard the
owls out there in the woods near my cabin. I knew
there were at least two from hearing them calling
(each other?) from separate directions. It was good
to hear them and I wanted them to stay.

The box I built I hung high on the trunk of a
birch tree – in accordance with the directions. It

9

remained vacant for two or three years. I knew they were still out there. I could hear them. I've had hours of enjoyment, laying awake nights with the cabin windows open, listening to them talking back and forth. "Who-cooks-for-you?" "Whoo-hoo-not-you" - words (sounds) to that effect. Sometimes they'll scream. Not often but, when they do it'll raise the hair on the back of your neck - even if you don't have hair on the back of your neck.

I have seen one of the owls several times (maybe both at different times?) down near the beaver pond. In season I would occasionally slip down quietly to try to catch a glimpse of the beaver as they came out for the evening. Sitting still and quiet in the fading light I might catch a movement - no sound, just movement - against the darkening sky. If I remained motionless the owl might perch in a nearby tree. It would lean one way - then the other. It would look directly at me. Its head would kind of go around, like the hand on a clock.

An owl's eyes are exceptionally sharp but myopic, nearsighted. They're immovable in the skull so it must move its head to look around.

The owl's hearing is exceptionally sharp. Sounds are somewhat amplified by the cupped shape of the feathers around its ears. Due to the offset placement of the ears (higher on one side of its skull than on the other), it senses direction of sounds with uncanny accuracy. A night hunter, it attacks in near total darkness. Direction is dictated almost exclusively by sound. Its feathers, unlike those of most birds, have a delicate fringe that enables the owl to fly silently. As it approaches its target, the "sound," last minute corrections refine the target area. The strike is made based entirely on where and what it hears. The victim doesn't know what's happening 'til it's too late. Owls don't often miss and their talons are deadly. They've been called the "Tigers of the Night."

Barred owls nest in January. The female incubates the eggs for about a month. The male brings her food during this period. Owls will eat anything from insects to small mammals. They swallow things whole. They don't have a digestion system like ours, no intestinal path to elimination. They'll digest what they have swallowed then regurgitate the indigestible parts - fur, bones feathers, etc. They'll eat a skunk too. That famous spray doesn't seem to have any effect on them.

There'll be two to four young born, eyes closed and down covered, requiring another month and a half to fledge, to fly. Both parents care for the young while this is happening.

Owls are territorial and will defend an area of 400 to 600 acres - a radius of about a half-mile. Sneaking up on an owl is harder than walking on water. With its sensitive hearing it probably heard the door slam when you left home back in town.

Slowly, quietly, carefully, and early each spring I stalked that nest box. I had no elusions I would be undetected, but I hoped the slow careful approach would not seem threatening. There were disappointments. The opening to the box always vacant - but wait! There! There, on the lip of the opening, fluttering faintly in a mere breath of moving air, was a single downy feather. It was small, almost tiny, but it shouted that something had brushed a feathered breast across the sawn opening.

I have sneaked back to look a couple times since that first discovery. I was fearful I might have chased them away. One day there was an owl - probably momma - in the box. She peered down at me, just the top half of her face showing. I didn't get too close and didn't stay long. I didn't come often either. It was enough to know that they were there. And then, one day, they were gone. I still hear them, now and again, on a still night. "Whoo, whoo, whoo-cooks-for-you?"

Indians have always felt a special relationship with animals. They seem to better appreciate their unique skills and abilities than the rest of us. They revere their "spirit." We could all learn something from that. A little respect is never misplaced.

Owls hold a special place in Indian culture. If you hear the owl call your name, you're going to die. It is the owl who guards the entrance to the milky way, that pathway of stars that all souls must follow to reach the spirit land. It guards the pathway to Heaven. Do you believe that? Those Indians are pretty foolish aren't they? The next thing they'll have someone rising from the dead.

Ω

Partridge

**Well suited to blending into their environment, the partridge
needs all the help it can get to survive. Who has not
experienced the sudden, explosive departure of this bird from
almost underfoot has not yet lived.**

Partridge

With fall's cold nights, cool days and a few
leaves prematurely turning color, comes a
premonition, a back-of-the-mind anticipation.
Something, something wonderful is coming.
Something enjoyable. Maybe a person takes special
notice as a brilliantly colored leaf drifts gently to the
ground. You're suddenly aware of the chill in the

13

morning air. Then it comes like a revelation! Fall! Golden forests! Frosty mornings! Partridge hunting season is fast approaching.

The aroma of Hoppe's #9 gun oil soon wafts through the house. Loving hands caress the comfortable feel of a familiar old shotgun. In the mind's eye is a picture of stalking along a familiar logging road, turning up a skidding trail, shotgun at the ready. Watching! Waiting! Listening for that most popular of all game birds: the ruffed grouse - partridge to most of us - "pats" to the "cool" hunters. This is hunting. A good and faithful bird dog is a joy to watch but not a necessity for enjoyment of the great outdoors in this most beautiful time of year. What pastime on earth is so invigorating, so enjoyable, or more nostalgic than a day spent in a golden sun-drenched autumn woods searching for that dumb but crafty, obvious but elusive, partridge?

The birds will be out at sunup, feeding. The frost stiffened leaves will crunch beneath your feet. Move slowly. Move quietly. Try to step where the leaves are not.

The birds will be searching here and there for food 'til about noon. Then they'll take a break, look up a familiar (to them) spot on an old tote road somewhere and dust themselves, to get rid of bugs, parasites. You and I might want to take a break too.

We'll stop at a spot I know. It's on the south side of a hill, in the sunshine, sheltered from the wind by a big rock. There's hot coffee in my thermos, a couple sandwiches in my game bag.

Donald Trump in his tower never enjoyed champagne and oysters on the half shell as much as we'll enjoy that coffee and those corned beef sandwiches. It'll be especially good if we start a small "lunch fire" and toast the sandwiches. That slightly smoky taste, maybe even burned just a little, that process adds is exquisite

After lunch, leaning against that rock in the warm sun, maybe you feel a nap coming on. Why not? The partridge are taking a break too. We'll pick up the action again later.

When we strike out again the frost is gone but the leaves are still noisy. We'll stay on the track of a logging road. The ground there is bare. No noise. Move slow and easy, watch, watch, and watch. Suddenly - whiiirrrrrr - and it's gone. It waited 'til you walked by and took off behind you, accelerating rapidly in low gear. That broad tail allows quick dodging and turning in the brush. By the time you turn and get your gun up, ole pat has arranged to have a tree between you. You stand alone and frustrated but with the memory - and the gun half way to your shoulder.

That bird stayed low and probably didn't fly more than two or three hundred yards. They rarely fly very far. But where did it go? Even if you saw it land you know it didn't stay there. A partridge is a walker, a fast walker. If you did see it flare and land, mark the spot carefully before you move. When you're sure you know where it landed start toward it - not too fast. It's probably run a ways already - maybe - but if you move slow, stay ready, you might get a quick shot if it takes off again. The chances are what, about fifty-fifty. Maybe you do, maybe you don't, but the adrenaline is flowing. Senses are alert. It's great to be this alive!

The population cycles of partridge can be dramatic. None one year and then, a couple years later, they're everywhere. A good indicator of their fall numbers is the past spring's weather conditions. The female lays and incubates 8 to 14 eggs between April and July. Incubation takes 23 or 24 days. The nest is on the ground and all sorts of predators have a taste for those eggs. Cold wet weather is a killer. Seven days after hatching the chicks are able to fly - 10 to 12 days later and they are roosting in trees. Owls, hawks, darn near all things that creep, crawl, or run - including house cats - are taking a toll as are disease and parasites. It's been said it takes 100 eggs laid to achieve three game birds but that seems a little overmuch. At that pace they'd soon be near extinction. An individual bird will probably live its whole life (it can be as long as 11 years) in an area encompassed by a circle of ½-mile radius.

About this time of year - early autumn - the birds experience a crazy time when they fly with wild and reckless abandon - everywhere - and run into anything: poles, wires, windows, automobiles - anything. It's about this time that the family breaks up. The Indians called it the time of the Mad Moon or Crazy Moon. Why? Who knows? Some say it's nature's way of preventing inbreeding. Maybe it's just that they're teenage about then.

Considering all the predators and problems it's not so strange that the bird's numbers get low. When the forests were cut down, when cities and people moved in, they adapted. They survived.

They give us a lot of enjoyment even those of us who don't get a shot. And when we do get one or two think of the road that bird traveled to get to your game bag. Show it a little appreciation, a little respect. And maybe you won't always take every shot you get.

♎

Come On Along

Porcupine

A porcupine assumes its defensive posture. Its head is tucked into the protective fence, prickly quills protect the body, and the tail is cocked and triggered to "flip" and imbed quills in anything foolish enough to venture close.

Porcupine

He (or she) wanders through the forest, seemingly unconcerned, winter and summer. Putting it kindly, I guess you'd have to say the Porcupine "doesn't count very fast." Its main interest in life is eating buds and twigs, almost anything green, and the inner bark of trees. It doesn't have sharp fangs or an aggressive disposition. It does have sharp claws for tree climbing but they're not very long. Otherwise it spends it time just waddling through life, usually at night, and minding its own business.

In late winter or early spring the "sap" rises - figuratively speaking - and the boy porcupines go in search of girl porcupines. Shortly thereafter from one to four (usually two) young are born. The young quickly develop quills of their own and learn the gait and tastes of their parents. They'll mature up to three feet long and weigh from fifteen to forty pounds

The porcupine creates a problem for loggers with his fondness for the inner bark of trees. He'll girdle a tree and/or its limbs thereby killing or deforming the tree, especially the young trees. Many of the old time "live-in-the-woods" lumberjacks had a soft spot for the porky calling it "the woodsman's friend." Being a slow creature it is easily caught and killed by a hungry man lost in the bush. Cooking amounts to a hot fire, bury the dearly departed "as-is" in the coals for about 30 minutes and - dinner is served!

Another irritating habit is the porky's taste for salt wherever it can find it. Many are the sweaty-handled axes whose owner has returned to find the handle chewed up.

My friend, Jud Cole, and I, as kids, were playing - I don't know, cowboys and Indians or something - when we came on a porcupine. We had sense enough not to get within range of the tail - instinct, I guess. A porcupine doesn't "shoot" its quills, you know. When angry or alarmed they'll raise them from their normally laid down position to their "don't mess with me" position. They'll poke their head in a hole or under a log or somewhere to protect their exposed face and rely on the quills and the lightning quick reflexes of that six-inch tail to discourage whatever's out there.

Anyway, our porky made it up a tree, a cluster of three or four young maples. I, being smarter than Jud (I thought), was up the tree right behind the porky with a pole in my hand. We must have been up that tree ten or fifteen feet - the porky four or five feet above me - and I'm poking at him with the stick. About the time the law of gravity, Newton and the apple you remember, registered in my quick (was Jud laughing at me?) mind the porky let go. Hot ziggedy dog! Well, he missed me on the way down through no fault of my own.

The porky wasn't hurt and wandered away. I wasn't hurt either and I wandered away too. You know, I do think Jud was laughing. It could easily have been a much more painful learning experience. Whenever I tell this story Jud still laughs!

A Veterinarian once told me he has dog-owner customers who come back again and again. The dogs don't seem to learn. The porky's quills release readily and have tiny barbs - "barbules" I believe they're called. They not only fasten the quill into flesh but any movement such as muscle contraction causes the quill to migrate deeper and deeper.

Those quills are the reason the porcupine is about the only "enemy" of a bear. The bear, being naturally curious and a bit playful, may cuff the porky in passing. The pain of the unexpected quills enrages the bear who may jump on or try to bite the porky. Definitely a bad idea. Painful quills lodged in the bear's mouth can lead to starvation. In many cases one or more quills migrate to vital organs and cause its demise. The pain and discomfort during this migration can only be imagined.

The same can be said for other unfortunate animals who attack a porcupine. Wolves and mountain lions, driven by hunger, have been known to tackle the porky. The results weren't always fatal but you can bet those critters were hungry.

The fisher, an animal of the weasel family approximately the size of a house cat, seems able to dine on porcupine without the perils of the quills. The fisher is extremely quick and agile. If the porky trees, the fisher swings under the branch and gets at the soft underbelly. In snow the fisher burrows under the snow to the belly - same result. If the fisher does catch a quill or two they don't seem to be a problem.

Aside from the fisher, automobiles are the porcupine's biggest hazard. When driving, watch for him. Unless you're awfully hungry, give him a break.

♎

Our Winter Fox Visitor

We live "in the suburbs," I guess you could say. There are houses on both sides and across the road but the rear faces a pond and marsh several hundred feet across. Lake Superior is just beyond. The marsh is where we first saw the fox. It isn't a place I'd normally expect to see a fox but there it was.

Trying to read tracks in the snow can be a guessing game. There are characteristics a person can learn and file away that narrow the odds but there will always be a degree of guessing. When you come right down to it - and this applies to life in general I guess - nobody really knows, everybody is guessing.

In this instance I knew that a fox has a rather small, dainty footprint. Its trail is neat and precise. Each track is precisely aligned with the others making a straight line. They'll place their rear foot where their front foot has been. Their tracks indicate they are generally going somewhere, unlike dogs that divert and circle and play around.

Seeing the tracks in the snow I guessed that a fox had made them. Actually seeing the fox making more tracks supported my assumption. There's no better way to learn tracking than seeing the animal making the tracks, then go examine them close up. The prints, the pattern, and the route the animal chose. It makes tracking next time a little easier.

23

You'll feel surer of your "guess."

This fox had come for the suet I had tossed out on the frozen bayou. The crows had gotten some of it but one chunk was too large for them to carry off. In the morning the suet was gone and there were the tracks of the fox.

The morning that we actually saw the animal the sun had just come up. The fox seemed to be enjoying itself and the beautiful sunrise by rolling in the snow and lying on a hummock. Maybe it was a bath of some sort? When Dorothy stepped out on the porch it stopped and, from a distance of 400 or 500 feet, just laid down in the snow in the morning sun and watched her. Its actions indicated a familiarity, confidence that it was sure of itself. We watched it. It watched us. I like to think we were all enjoying the morning.

The red fox is not native to North America. It was brought over from Europe - probably England - around 1700 to provide sport for early settlers. Fox have provided hunting entertainment for horsemen (and women) riding to the hounds since away back in the 1300s. "Tally ho!" and all that rot, you know. The chase was the thing, not the killing. George Washington is said to have enjoyed fox hunting.

Tales of a fox's cunning border the animal on genius. Aesops Fables extolling the wisdom of the fox date back to 600 BC. A fox (one or more?) once took a pack of hounds on a three-day junket finally losing them in an area about 40 miles from their beginning. The hunters on that hunt wound up hunting for their dogs rather than the fox.

Actually a fox is pretty much a family animal. It enjoys a life span of eight to ten years – if it's lucky. It will weigh 8 to 14 pounds and measure about 40 inches long (including a 14 inch tail). Breeding season is February through May, gestation is 49-52 days, and the kits - from three to ten - are born blind in a den. After nine days, their eyes are open. Both male and female care for the young. The kits begin to leave the den after eight or ten weeks. The family stays together 'til early fall.

A fox's range is generally five or six miles. It's nocturnal, resting during the day. The den is for raising young and rarely used after that. They often return to the same den each year. They are fond of favorite loafing spots - like wolves - where they sun themselves and rest. Their tail – a "brush," it's called - is an important part of its anatomy. It's a blanket or muff to cover the feet, the nose, and for protection and warmth while it rests or sleeps.

It eats mice, rabbits, squirrels, birds, insects including grasshoppers, and darn near anything else including fruits and berries. It's enemies include wolves, coyote, bobcat, lynx, fisher and - depending a lot on the demands of style and fur pieces - man.

He finally tired of watching and vanished over a sand dune. Since we're not raising livestock or chickens the fox isn't a problem. I like seeing it. I hope it stays. I've got more suet.

Ω

Come On Along

Photo courtesy of John "Jim" Wohlfiel.

Black Bear

A black bear in a posture that looks like you or I. It's difficult to see but there's a fish hanging from that tree about two feet from his nose.

The Bear and I

The sun was low in the west at our little cabin in the woods. Shadows shrouded the glass-smooth water of a little pond created by a beaver dam. It was nestled in a shallow valley dug by a small creek. Sitting quietly on a bench I had built I watched the smooth surface of the water. Dug into the far bank was the den of the beaver. I watched for any ripples on the surface. Any slight movement of the water would indicate that the beaver, a nocturnal animal, had come out to begin

27

its evening activities. Dorothy and I had been living in the woods near this beaver dam for a couple years now. We try to avoid bothering the beaver but we do slip down now and then just to see if the beaver are still there.

This particular evening I watched and waited, quiet and motionless. Time passed. The shadows deepened. Suddenly I felt the presence of someone behind me - you know the feeling. I thought Dorothy might have come to join me watching. I slowly turned my head, not wanting to spook the beaver if it were out. There - right behind me sniffing at my hip pocket - was a black bear.

The bear noticed my movement and pulled back. Startled we looked at each other at a distance of three or four feet. Time stood still. The bear snorted and ran maybe 30 feet. It stopped, turned, and sat down. We just looked at each another. Neither of us moved.

Our cabin sits in the woods by the Yellow Dog River in Michigan's Upper Peninsula. It used to be called the Yellow Dog Hunting and Fishing Club. Before that it belonged to Tom "Tin Can" Sullivan, a local legend in his time. More recently, Dad and I and our "bunch" used to spend the first week or so of deer hunting season up here. We enjoyed the hunt, the cabin, the woods, and mostly the camaraderie of a group of men with a common interest. We were carpenters, electronic experts, aviators, policemen, salesmen, a doctor, a mechanic, but we all shared an enjoyment of the outdoors. A hunting license in those days was for deer, a buck (with four inch or better antlers), and/or a black bear.

Sometimes we got several deer - plus a "camp deer" which was allowed in those days. There was only once I remember someone getting a bear - and that memory is vague. Some years we didn't shoot anything - got "skunked" as they say. Ah, but nobody really cared. No one who spent time with that bunch ever got "skunked." There were compensations. There was Redge's cooking (excellent), Don pulling off a practical joke (Redge thought he, Don, was a bear in the dark), a strange yowl Arvid and I heard (It came from a deer stand I had just walked away from).

We use to attract a few deer evenings with apples or a little stale bread scattered around in an open area by the cabin. We didn't shoot them. We simply fed them. After chasing them around all day, it seemed fair. There was no "baiting" allowed back in those days - not even a salt block. These are all delicious memories. The smell of wet wool socks hung over the stove. The slap of playing cards dealt by lantern light. Watching the sunrise over a silent forest from atop the rocks west of the cabin. Toasting a sandwich over an open fire in the bush. Lying on your belly for a drink of water from a small stream - water so cold it hurt your teeth. Watching a squirrel burrow in the leaves for acorns - sounding like a herd of elephants coming down the draw. Ah, those were the days, my friend. We thought they'd never end. . . ."

But they did end. People grow older; move away, friendships change. There are more and more people building cabins in what was once our vast empty forest. Hunting techniques have faded away to be replaced by baiting and hunting blinds. Inviting something to dinner and then shooting it as it sits down to eat just rubs me the wrong way. It's quicker and easier - but it's wrong. Maybe it's this "instant gratification" society we seem to have become? Maybe it's Democrats in the Whitehouse? Whatever it is we don't seem to have the time to enjoy the hunt. We get the game to come to us - and stand there. All we have to do is shoot them! And we don't want just one. We want to shoot the first one, well, because that's what you're supposed to do when you're hunting. And then we want to shoot another one. With that second one we'll be selective, we'll only shoot a real "trophy." But then there's another season - muzzle loading - and there's bow season. We should be able to shoot another one then - for each of the seasons - or maybe we could shoot two? If we get one on opening day, what'll we do for the rest of the season?

Bear hunting has become another problem. The licensing selection process is like winning the lottery. In the old days everybody used to have a bear-hunting license. It came with the deer-hunting license but you had to go look for the bear, not bait them. That system didn't make bear an endangered species. Bear are not creatures of habit in the way that deer are. Bear roam far and wide. In the fall, in preparation for hibernation, something kicks in and the bear becomes a glutton, a regular food junkie. It'll eat and eat and eat voraciously. When it finds a source of food, it'll eat, sleep, eat, and stay in that area 'til the food is gone. If the food is replaced, the bear will keep coming back. It's such a successful system that today's hunters-over-bait must be limited by the lottery system so they don't kill all the bear.

A couple professors over in Minnesota have come up with a theory on "Stages of Hunting." You've gotta be careful when you're dealing with "professors." They're smart! Listen to them when they talk. But keep your own council. If you hang around in those ivory towers of academia you tend to get weird. Anyway, those professors divided "hunting" into five stages:

The "Shooter" stage is usually the beginners. When they start hunting, they want a lot of shooting. Birds, rabbits, chipmunks, tin cans - whatever - just so there's a lot of shooting. Probably a lot of missing too - it doesn't matter.

The second stage is the "Limiting Out" stage. In involves lots of shooting but lots of hitting too. Shooting well enough to limit out the license with the game taken.

The third stage is the "Trophy" stage. Here the hunter specializes! They've had enough of just "limiting out" and are now out to get the king-of-the-hill to mount on the wall.

The fourth stage is the "Method" stage. These hunters buy all the bells and horns and whistles in the equipment category - and only the best. Hunting for them has become an important part of life, a challenge. It's a kind of "one on one" contest - but a very one-sided contest. "If I win, you're dead! If you win, well, you don't really win - you just don't lose." These hunters may even place limitations on themselves - using a bow and arrow or black powder muzzle-loading rifle for example. It elevates the challenge. The only one this method is really hard on is the game. Unless the hunter has honed his killing skill, the game may escape with wounds that can impair or kill them slowly and painfully.

The fifth stage of hunting is called the "Mellowed Out" stage. These hunters are usually the older, more seasoned hunters. The "killing" part may still be there but it's not so important. The enjoyment now is taken from the splendor of the forest, the depth of the hunting experience, the camaraderie of the hunting camp, and the challenge of lining up a probable killing shot – then not taking the shot. There's an admiration and appreciation of the quarry, and a vague realization of the almost mystical unity of all living things.

Is that what you and I are sharing, Mr. Black Bear that "mystical unity" thing? Maybe there's something to that? Something I've noticed about you, Mr. Bear, that is - what shall I call it? - unsettling I guess. If I kill you and skin you out - -

you look an awful lot like me. And if you kill me - well - let's don't go there.

What else might we share, you and I? Here's a toast to you my friend, before we part: May we both live, love, and laugh each day as if it were our last - for one day we'll be right! And we share that, too, you and I. The bear evidently tired of all this philosophical tom-foolery. He glanced briefly toward the cabin - maybe Dorothy had dropped a pan or something - then slowly rose, looked at me once, and ambled off.

As I turn my attention back to the pond I notice a ripple on the water. There he is, the beaver! Glad you're still around. I slowly get to my feet and carefully and quietly walk back to the cabin.

Ω

Come On Along

The Cabin Mouse

It's fall in the north woods. Our little cabin up along a remote section of the Yellow Dog River has seen many seasons come and go. It stands stoically against wind and rain and snow and sunshine for – well, for more years than I have. A fella' named Tom "Tin-Can" Sullivan came into this area in 1923 when the area was a lot wilder and more remote. He had been living in a little shack the other side of the river, over by the old Laurich farm. Before that he'd been down around Seney, a pretty wild little lumber town east of Munising some forty or fifty miles from here. He'd been a bartender, some say. Before that – well, folks back then made a point of not looking too far into someone's past.

Tom built a cabin on this site in 1923. A forest fire burned him out in 1927. He built again and this is the place we now call our "huntin' camp." There were a bunch of "good ole' boys" who had bought it from Tom's estate. Over the years friendships changed, people moved away, some died, and finally my father and I wound up with it. Dad has gone on to that great deer stand in the sky and now it's just mine. Yes, this old cabin has seen a lot of seasons come and go.

When you haven't lived in a place for a while - especially a place way back in the woods - somebody or something else will probably move in.

35

I try to stop by occasionally to keep an eye on the place, to "check things out." A visit never fails to stir emotions. There are so many happy memories suspended in the dust of that musty, dim interior. It's kind of sad to see the "empty."

It's not really empty though. The ceiling has a layer of dead leaves I once stowed up there as insulation. Those leaves have attracted squirrels looking for a warm winter home. A weasel called it home for a season or two. A local skunk moves in under the floor now and then. There are no problems, no odors. The skunk's a good tenant. Usually there are mice! Mice are everywhere in the woods, not just in the cabin. They're exceptionally prolific and provide a ready food source for everything carnivorous. I guess that's their place in the great scheme of things.

Over the years, coming and going to this cabin, I've learned to live with the mice - after a fashion. We haven't become intimate or anything but we grow comfortable with one another. They rustle through the leaves over the ceiling and run across the cabin floor. In the evening they'll scurry from one hiding place to another. There's at least one of them who'll sometimes pause in the doorway to the kitchen, just beside the fireplace. Its head will move one way - and then the other. Its nose wiggles. Its eyes are steady on me - checking me over. It's like he's greeting me, kind of a "How ya doin'? Welcome to my pad" sort of thing.

Late one night while I was sleeping a mouse -

I guess it was a mouse– ran right across my face, down my arm, and was gone. It woke me up but whatcha gonna do? I guess I could have hollered and jumped up and groped around in the dark 'til I could finally turn on a flashlight, but then what? The mouse (or whatever it was) isn't about to stop for pictures. I thought about it – maybe five seconds - then rolled over and went back to sleep. My brother-in-law was at the cabin that night too. When morning broke I awoke and looked around and he wasn't in his bunk? I looked some more, wondering if he had made one of those necessary trips to the outhouse. I waited, watched, and finally went outside. And then I found him. He was outside - sleeping in the bed of his pickup truck. He hadn't taken kindly to those mice and their nocturnal partying. There must have been a swinging time in mouseville last night.

When Dorothy and I stayed at the camp Dorothy used to carry on a "search and destroy" war with them. She ran a trap line and even kept score on how many mice she caught. I was the one, however, who was called upon to empty the traps. It didn't cause me any trauma but I have to admit to a twinge of regret wondering if each one of them might be my buddy from the kitchen doorway. I gave them all a suitable burial (tossed them into the woods) and hoped that some other creature might benefit from their demise.

When summer faded away Dorothy and I prepared to vacate our palace in the pines for our annual motor home trek to the warmer climes of our southern and/or southwestern states. The day we were leaving, closing the cabin for the winter, I chanced to open a seldom-used drawer in the kitchen. I pulled it out a bit beyond its normal travel. There, away in the back, was a nest maybe eight inches square. It filled a corner of the three or four inch deep drawer. I recognized much of the nesting materials. There were feathers from a partridge that'd crashed through a window that spring. There's a kind of "crazy time" in the spring of year when partridge just jump and fly into windows and all sorts of things. It lay on the floor for a few days until we returned. There were also a few threads from the curtains, yarn from an afghan, flannel from an old shirt. Beside the nest was maybe a quart and a half of seeds gathered from bird feeders, the grass, and wherever else mice find seeds. There were even some peanuts, some sunflower seeds, and others I didn't recognize. The mouse had a well-stocked larder for the coming winter season.

I paused to examine this little hideaway. A quick glance around showed that Dorothy was out at the truck. "Geeez," I thought. "If she sees this she'll have a fit." No matter that we'll be gone for the winter. I'd better clean it out and just not say anything.

Sliding the drawer all the way out I carried it out the back door and over to the edge of the woods. I was just about to toss the whole thing into the brush when a little head popped out of the feathers and threads. It stared right at me, wiggled its whiskers and seemed to say, "Hi, Ben. How ya doin'? You remember me, dontcha? From over by the fireplace? Are you all ready for winter? I think it's gonna be a cold one." Aaaw shucks! What do I do now?

I looked at that little mouse. The mouse looked at me. It wasn't afraid of me. It made no attempt to jump out of the drawer or run away. It just looked at me – right in the eye.

I looked up at the bare trees. This was November in northern Michigan. Snow and cold and ice were just around the corner. If I tossed that nest and those seeds away there wouldn't be time for the mouse to build a new nest and replace his larder. I was holding its survival in my hands. We just looked at each other. It knew – and I knew - and I just couldn't do it.

I glanced around again, looking toward our pickup truck. Dorothy wasn't watching me. Surreptitiously I slunk back into the cabin. I carefully lined up the drawer and slid it gently back into the cabinet. All the while the mouse watched me. As it slid under the lip of the table the mouse ducked its head, still watching. I stopped.

Dorothy called from the truck. "Ben? Where are you? Are you ready to go?"

That mouse and I looked each other, right in the eye. I swear that mouse winked at me. "If Dorothy finds out about this," I said, "we're both dead." (Did that mouse nod or was that my imagination?) "Don't you say anything, little mouse. I won't either. But by next spring you'd better be gone." I gently slid the drawer closed.

"Yeah, honey," I called. "I'll be right there."

"Let's go," she replied impatiently.

"Yup! All cleaned up, locked up, and ready to go." I called back. I paused and looked at that closed drawer. Good luck, little mouse.

♎

Autumn

As summer fades the sun slowly recedes southward, leaves begin to turn color. There are several explanations offered but I suspect that no one really knows - everyone's guessing.

A popular pastime is trying to predict when the color will "peak." It's a fool's errand really. There are too many variables of wind and weather. We're better advised to simply be aware that it is happening and enjoy it each day that goes by.

A cold breath of wind may intrude now and then foretelling the icy blast of winter just around the corner. But Indian summer with its balmy southern breeze caresses the observer seductively as he or she stretches out on a sunny hillside soaking up the warm. Mice and chipmunks and beaver will have laid up a goodly supply of food to see them through the winter. Bear will soon feel that irresistible urge to gorge themselves in preparation for their winter hibernation. Deer will experience the urge to mate, to procreate as the nights grow colder. The bucks with their resplendent antlers will vie with one another for a lady's favor before the snow forces them all into the swamps and heavy cover to hunker up and survive 'til spring.

It's a time to enjoy but be prepared.

♎

Come On Along

Mallard Duck

A soon-to-be southbound duck wings into our bayou for a little feed corn we've scattered to sustain him on the trip

Listen to the Weather

On the shore of Lake Superior in Michigan's Upper Peninsula summer drifted by lazily, effortlessly, almost unnoticed. But now there was no question in mid September of what the changing weather was telling us. The wind had swung around to the north. The temperature went down – and down. The skies turned a dark, heavy gray. Driving rain sheeted against the windows and sizzled into the waters of the bayou. Big northern pine trees leaned ponderously, rocking with the gusts, accepting the onslaught with a heavy sigh. Rainwater gushed from the roof to the gutters and tumbled all over itself as it fell to the deck below. This scene of things to come sent me scurrying to the basement to check the furnace filter, the pilot light, and then to bump up the thermostat.

The north wind driving the water toward the south shore has caused the level in Lake Superior to rise. The wind and waves have the Chocolay River backing up, having trouble emptying into the lake. The river level at the Green Bay Street bridge was up a foot or more.

Our squirrels and chipmunks took cover early on. One or two brave chickadees performed an aerial dance to catch a swaying perch on the bird feeder. Typical of the chickadee, they snatch a sunflower seed and quickly flit away to a tree branch to open and eat it.

The weather didn't seem to bother the ducks at all. Ducks are like the fighter pilots of the waterfowl world, darn near all-weather fighter pilots too. When they arc in from the lake with that wind behind them they look like General Chuck Yeager breaking the sound barrier. Our bayou seems to be a popular stopping place.

I've gotten in the habit of feeding the ducks, tossing whole corn into the shallows near our boat dock. The ducks are often waiting at first light for me to serve breakfast. I'll fill a cut-off half-gallon plastic milk container with whole corn, brave the wind and rain on the exposed porch, and throw - hard - against the wind. Most of it makes it to the water. A little lands on the bank but they'll get that too.

The ducks used to fly off when I came out.

Later they would just paddle clear of the falling corn, nervously hold their position, and quickly return to feed. Now they'll be jockeying each other for position while the corn is still in the air.

After braving the elements I'd quickly retreat to shelter inside. Then I'd stand, coffee mug in hand, watching the ducks dabble and dive and argue with one another. When they finish they move back offshore, tuck their head under their wing and sleep, I guess. They make themselves right at home, weather and all. Come to think of it, they are at home. Their feathers and underlying down must be very efficient waterproof insulation. It's hard to accept that they're warm, dry, and comfortable out there.

Out on Lake Superior an ore boat swings at anchor just off shore. I guess it's buttoned down to ride out this stretch of bad weather. I wonder what the crew is doing? Somebody is undoubtedly on watch. Others are probably reading, sleeping, watching TV. Maybe one of them is standing at a porthole, coffee cup in hand, looking at my house and wondering what I'm doing.

Those boats are a community unto themselves during· the shipping season. On days like this I imagine the shadow of the Edmund Fitzgerald disaster falls across their thoughts. "Big Fitz" was a community too - swallowed whole by the waves of this inland sea. Lake Superior can be terribly unforgiving and should never be taken lightly.

All day the waves, the "White Horses" of the

breakers, march steadily, relentlessly onto the shore. Encountering a breakwater or a rocky coastline they will explode into spray destroying themselves in a seemingly fruitless attack on an immovable force. Ah, but know that over time they will wear down the hardest of obstacles. The persevering waves will triumph. Time is on their side.

The sun slowly slips below the horizon. Across the bay lights blink on one by one in the city of Marquette. Deck lights of the ore boat glow in the fading light. As darkness thickens the rotating beam of the lighthouse sweeps the ragged skirts of low hanging clouds. It's time for bed.

The rain is perpetual. The gusting wind rattles a loose board somewhere. Raindrops rattle against the bedroom window. The headlights of a passing car flash into the room momentarily illuminating details. Then darkness returns, seemingly even deeper than before. Gradually the sounds of the tempest blend into a sort of lullaby. They begin to fade, receding farther and farther away until they merge into a deep sleep. Tomorrow will be better.

Ω

The Ole Mud Hole

The ole mud hole. Not an uncommon encounter when traveling the back roads of the north country

Come On Along

Autumn in the Woods

The mailbox flag is down. There are fresh tire tracks on the side of the road. The mail delivery has been here. There are two bills and a letter from Dorothy's daughter. It could have been worse. It could have been three bills.

It's a couple and a half miles from the cabin to the mailbox beside the county road. I try to walk that distance often. It's good exercise. The weather doesn't always cooperate though. Cold rain is falling today. Snowflakes have been reported in a small town just to the west. When an air mass moves south across the broad expanse of Lake Superior it picks up moisture, "lake effect" it's called locally, and drops it on the land area of upper Michigan as rain - or snow.

Fall winds bluster and gust through the trees stripping the brightly colored leaves. The forest floor becomes a multi-colored shag carpet. The gentle summer shades and shadows, the gaily nodding trilliums and the soft breezes are gone. Trees will soon be left standing, naked and exposed, their bare limbs extended toward the gray October sky. They don't beg or plead or ask why. They simply accept the inevitable. It's a somber thing - kind of like a funeral.

It's fall in upper Michigan, late fall. There will be periods of Indian summer yet to come but time is growing short. I hunch up my shoulders, turn up the collar of my heavy coat and walk on. The old two-track logging road I'm following leads to my snug little cabin near the Yellow Dog River north of Marquette.

While I was growing up, this place didn't hold much attraction for me. It wasn't where the "action" was. It's still not where the "action" is. That's why it attracts me now. The conditions out here are beautifully consistent! There's nothing devious or convoluted about the place. What you see is what you get. I sometimes feel it's one of the few honest and straightforward places left in this world. If you get tangled up between a she bear and her cub she's very apt to kill you. The rules are simple and unencumbered by obfuscated explanations. Here is true equality. Everything receives the same treatment. I love it! I respect it. And at times I'm a little afraid of it – which is a healthy approach.

I tuck the mail safely in an inside pocket. The rain has slowed to a sort of drizzle. As I walk back along the old road I come to a stand of white birch trees that overlook Bear Lake. It's a favorite spot of mine. Autumn leaves cover the ground, wet and forlorn looking. Even in the rain this is a beautiful spot. I stop for a bit to reminisce and admire the view.

There's a bar of soap hidden under a piece of bark in an old tree stump near the lake. This is a good place for a person living alone in the woods to take a bath - in the warm sun of summer, of course. It's a bit cool today. I'll leave the soap where it is. It'll still be there next summer.

One fall some years ago my son, Benny, and his friend wanted to camp out among these birch trees on the shore of the lake - by themselves. The boys were in their early teens and were feeling the urge to be independent. They had a pup tent, hatchets, hunting knives, waterproof matches, camping kits (you know the kind –aluminum – with those cups that burn your lips) and a couple of those little fold up knife/fork/spoon rigs).

"Can we, Dad?"

"Sure!"

Later that night I made two trips - covertly - through the black-dark woods to see how they were doing. I had visions of them chopping a leg or burning a hand or starting a forest fire. All seemed OK. The boys had things well in hand. They were having a great time. I stayed hidden and they never knew I had been there. I got whole lot of mosquito bites and barked shins and not much sleep for my trouble that night. Would I do it again? Sure I would! So would you. Memories are made of this.

A little farther on there's a large mud hole in the trail. It's right where another side road turns off and it's been there for as long as I can remember. It dries out during the summer but it's there again every spring and every fall - and after a heavy rain. That mud hole has memories too. It's been a landmark to those of us who are a part of the

"Natural Elusion" and for others who frequently use the Bushy Creek Truck Trail. A person might describe a location as "just west of the old mud hole," you know, like that. My Dad and I used to come up for deer hunting when the cabin was called "The Yellow Dog Hunting and Fishing Club." The old mud hole was an item to contend with and a topic of conversation. "Did you make 'er through the ole mud hole?" was a common greeting when you would arrive.

Dad had a 1936 Oldsmobile in those days. We'd always build up speed for the rush at that formidable expanse of water and mud. The punishment that old Oldsmobile took slipping and spinning and lurching and bucking its way through that hole would put modern four-wheelers to shame. That old car was built of some kind of strong steel. Unfortunately it didn't always make it through. That's when we turned to muscle and bone and ropes and pulleys and pry poles and brush - brush which seemed to disappear into that bottomless hole. I picked up a little language that falls in the "Don't say that in front of your Mother" category at that ole mud hole. Oh, well, the mud washed off.

The Department of Natural Resources - maybe it was the Conservation Department back then? Anyway, they came up the trail one year in response to a forest fire. With their mechanized equipment they filled in the old mud hole a bit so they could pass more easily. That bit of fill and my present-day four-wheel drive truck have diminished the terrors of the ole mud hole. It's still there though and so are the memories. It's funny, isn't it, how fall seems to be a time of memories. I can't suppress a grin as I skirt the puddle and continue along the trail.

I wasn't being very observant as I plodded along putting one foot in front of the other. I was thinking of a warm fireplace at the end of the trail. Rounding a bend I approach an old apple orchard. I often wondered who planted those trees? They're old. It must have been a long time ago.

The old orchard is located at a choice spot on a piece of flat land about 30 feet above the Yellow Dog River. A part of the Bushy Creek Truck Trail used to pass along the base of the hill. Early one spring the river shifted its course a bit and the rest of us had to shift our course too. It washed out a section of our road.

Some beaver once selected the site as a possible location for a dam. They took down several large aspen trees and did manage to back up two or three feet of water. The volume of flow and the force of the Yellow Dog River were too much though. They were never able to close the center section of their dam. Subsequent springs have since washed away all but a few of the chewed-up stumps.

The wind and rain have let up but it's still gray and overcast. Suddenly I am aware of a shape, a shape standing very still under a distant tree. I stopped dead in my tracks. It's a deer, ears at attention, standing there watching me. Nothing moves for several seconds. On a nearby tree a drop of water, falling from a high branch strikes a leaf lower down. The leaf flinches and its small branch quivers. The deer and I continue watching each other. The deer suddenly looks away, ears homing in on some new sound in the wet forest. There are no antlers. It looks back at me. I haven't moved. Then it turns and in one beautifully fluid motion leaps away, white flag flashing for several jumps before it disappears. I am left looking at the empty spot where it had stood. Beautiful! Ah, well, again one foot in front of the other I slog on. .

Tom Sullivan had lived up here in the 1920s with kerosene lamps and a wood stove. I wonder what he would think if he could look at his cabin now, especially the television? I've put in several windows since then too. Toms "decor" was sort of "early American bear's den." Otherwise it's the same place ole Tom built back in 1927. The 2 x 4s in the walls measure a true 2" x 4," something I discovered when I was installing the windows. Some have said Tom got the nickname "Tin Can" from the tin cans that accumulated around the cabin. Rusty cans and old bottles can still be found - no aluminum, just tin. I don't know if they're Tom's tin cans or not. I prefer to believe another story I heard from some of the old timers who remembered Tom. Tom had an expression he applied to organizations that weren't as efficient as he thought they should be. He called them "tin-can outfits."

54

Tom died back in 1928 –or was it '29? He just got tired of living, I guess. Maybe he was bored -or discouraged -or maybe just drunk? Anyway, he shot himself right here in the cabin. They were some kind of men, those guys who lived in the brush and cut the big pines. I'm a tenant in your cabin, Tom, and I thank you. I hope whoever comes along after me will have the good fortune of knowing about who built the place -warts and all.

Come on along with me, Tom. Let's go watch the leaves turn color and feel the nip of arctic air as it slips down from Canada. We'll watch the deer feeding on the apples under the trees you planted beside the cabin. These are things that never change, Tom, the things that are "true." This old place is a mental decongestant for me, for the complexities of today's world. I just have this strong urge to get up here every now and then.

I'm almost in sight of the cabin. I catch the smell of wood smoke on the damp heavy air. That's another memory jogger - another of my favorite things. There's a warm cozy campfire in the cabin and I'll soon --. Whumpumpumpumpump!

A partridge suddenly explodes into the air right beside me. Adrenalin floods my system. I'm ready to run off in several directions all at the same time. Damn! They scare-a-person-near-to-death! Those partridge never seem to get out of low gear.

We have either seen several partridge or the same bird several times since we've been here. It's nice to have them around. I wish they'd announce themselves a bit more gently though. No! No, I don't really wish that at all. I want them to be just what they are.

The days have grown shorter, almost unnoticed but inevitably so. They used to say it was the cold that caused the leaves to change colors. Now they say it's the decreasing length of daylight. It causes the tree to withhold nutrients from its leaves, a sort of drawing within in anticipation of the coming winter. I don't know what does it - or why. Does it really matter? I'm always awed by the results.

The sunny days of Indian summer, the soft breezes, the gloriously riotous colors create an ambience without equal anywhere. The mood is narcotic. The woodland creatures with experience, the survivors, are starkly aware that this seductive sedation will be followed swiftly by a merciless onslaught of ice and snow and arctic cold. Prepare! There will be no second chance. Who is not prepared will not survive. It's another of the consistencies, the honesty of this natural world. 'Seems like that's kind of "profound?" It's like I am on the verge of knowing some great eternal truth or something? I guess I'm just not smart enough to be able to make it out.

I did cut a shed full of firewood. Dorothy and I won't be staying here thru the winter, but there's something -call it an instinct -that compels me to cut firewood.

My father had a thing about wood - especially firewood. He was raised in a 12 by 20 foot frame house just north of Calumet on Upper Michigan's Keweenaw Peninsula, in an area called Lakeview. His father, my grandfather, worked underground in a copper mine. The family also had 40 acres on which they grew vegetables and things. I've been up to Lakeview. The thing that grows most handily on that hillside is rocks. In that small house dad had lived with his mother and father, two brothers, three sisters and a couple cousins. It was a wood frame house, wood heated it, and wood cooked their meals. They probably sold a little wood too. Wood was important to them - it was essential. I guess my instinct harkens back to that. I guess it's a genetic thing.

Fortunately there's a lot of firewood around our little cabin. There are many small maples from a couple inches to four or five inches in diameter. And there's deadwood, trees crowded out by stronger neighbors. Gathering these deadfalls a person can't help but explore the tracks and trails. Some are heavily overgrown and haven't been used for many years. They aren't readily apparent to the casual observer. They only show as a six or eight foot reasonably flat area that winds through the woods. They're broken up by overgrown washouts and obscured by brush. Trees have sprung up and matured in the track. There've been many snows since white pine logs rode frozen skid-ways down these trails. They're fading away. The eternal truth: "this, too, shall pass."

My boots thump loudly on the boards of the porch. I shuffle my feet in a futile attempt to dislodge the wet leaves. Dorothy has a hot cup of coffee waiting for me. She saw me coming up the trail.

The wet boots come off and are stood to dry beside the hot Franklin stove. Not too close though. They're old boots, heels run down, leather uppers scarred and sagging in folds, especially around the ankles. I've walked many miles in those boots - those old comfortable boots.

The nights are getting colder, especially the clear nights. First one up in the morning makes the fire. Dorothy sure has cold feet when she jumps back into bed. She's planted some daffodils and crocus around the cabin. Those early flowers will be nice in the spring. She put some chicken wire over the bulbs in the flowerbed trying to keep the critters out. The squirrels and the chipmunks like bulbs too - not the flowers just the bulbs. Maybe they enjoy the flowers too? Who am I to say?

I had built several birdhouses which are now in trees here and there, visible from the windows. Maybe they'll have tenants in the spring?

The first snow is beautiful. It crept in quietly one night. It's a soft white blanket that forms lace trim on naked branches and smoothes the forest floor. Fresh tracks show where a squirrel dug for sunflower seeds and where the birds have been foraging. The open fireplace fire feels especially good these frosty mornings.

A thin sheet of ice covers our rain barrel. There's a snug feeling of security in the knowledge that there's wood in the box and food on the shelf. A person doesn't have to face the ice and snow. Not for a while anyway.

It's exciting to experience the first snowfall while in the woods. It doesn't normally stay for long. It's like a scout out ahead of the main force. You know there's more coming. The camp is a safe haven. A person can observe the advance of winter from a secure position near the fireplace. It's important to be aware that a sudden storm can close the trails, bury them in snow. Your choices then are limited. Stay where you are or abandon the vehicles and retreat – run - back to thermostatically controlled central heating, thick insulation, and electric lights.

We choose not to tempt the fickle goddess of meteorology. I've seen the cavalier way she treats her high priests of weather forecasting. We will gather our meager belongings and retire from the field while we're still able to choose.

So long, Tom. Take care of the place. There's a family of squirrels living in the leaves that insulate the ceiling, you know. And there's a partridge just down the road a ways. The deer are around too, of course.

Oh! say, Tom, the moose are back! Have you heard? They flew some of them in from Canada.

My brother-in-law saw one a couple weeks ago up on the Pesheekee grade. How about that? I wish they'd try again with the wolves. You used to hunt the wolves, for bounty, remember? Now you're both gone. I wonder where the rest of us are headed?

♎

A Scream in the Dark

This story goes back a few hunting seasons - and it's probably gotten better as the years go by. No matter! It was a pretty good story to start with.

It happened during the first few days of upper Michigan's deer hunting season. Our regular gang had gathered at our Palace in the Popples. We all had stalked the woods, watched, waited, and tried to out figure the deer. Profound thought and philosophical pronouncements flowed freely. No one had yet shot nor even shot at a deer but no one was overly concerned. Redge, the camp cook, was outdoing himself as usual providing culinary delights, each meal surpassing the one before. The old woodstove was fired up keeping us warm and drying our socks. The coffee was hot. The weather was beautiful. Life was good.

This particular evening, about an hour before sunset and our evening meal, Arvid and I decided to hike out west of camp a half mile or so. There were a couple of likely spots that just might produce an evening deer. We'd planned to just sit and watch 'til dark. Maybe one of us would get lucky. There were several oak trees in the spot I chose, the ground was still bare, and - well - who knows?

I had a place in mind under an old hemlock tree. I'd made "lunch camp" there a few times and had a comfortable seat rigged up. Arvid chose a low pine tree on a ridge overlooking a likely deer run. He was about a quarter mile closer to camp. We took our positions and watched and waited, silent as the sphinx.

All was quiet, still, tranquil, in the evening woods. In the silent splendor of fall in the northern woods it was like being in church. A person could sit in that serenity and communicate with the eternal.

Suddenly there was a thunderous thrashing and crashing! It came from behind the rocks, up the hill on my right. My first thought was buffalo, a herd of buffalo stampeding down the draw. I raised my rifle, prepared to sell my life dearly. Closer they came charging around a large rock. I sighted down the barrel at - a squirrel? A red squirrel was charging through the dry leaves scratching and digging and leaping about. He seemed to be searching for acorns. Phew! OK, little fella', I'm gonna be looking for something to eat myself before long. The thrashing fades as the squirrel moves away and once more took to the trees.

Time passes slowly, tranquilly. The sun silently slips lower and lower and finally disappears. The squirrel has not returned, gone wherever it is that squirrels go. The scene was slowly losing its contrast. What had once been sharp features were now blending, fading into grays and blacks and shadow. It was one of those times you wish wouldn't end – but of course it does, gradually fading away. Nothing is forever. Finally I could no longer see my gun-sights - or much else for that matter.

After one more long, slow, and careful check all around I gradually got to my feet. Walking slowly and as quietly as I could I moved toward Arvid's stand some 1,200 or 1,500 feet away. It must have taken me ten minutes or so to get there.

"Ya seen anything?" Arvid asked speaking softly, still looking, watching, listening.

I shook my head.

"Me neither." We stood peering into the gathering gloom for a minute or so

I shrugged. "Whaddya say we . . ."

"SCREEEEYOWWWLL!" The hair stood straight up on the back of my neck. That scream had come from where I had just been sitting.

I looked at Arvid. He looked at me. Both of us stood, wide eyed, white knuckled, gripping our guns. Each of us tried to look in all directions at once. Suddenly the woods seemed darker.

"What wuzzat?"

Arvid shook his head, "I dunno."

Silence! Nothing!

"Let's head back to camp."

"OK."

And we didn't fool around along the way either.

Back at the cabin we shared our experience with the others. Speculation ranged from the profound to the ridiculous; a bobcat, an owl, a panther, a ghost. No one really knew.

After silently listening to the rambling

discussion Arvid stood up, stretched, and spoke. "I know what happened."

That got everyone's attention.

I finally broke the pregnant silence. "What? what happened?"

"Well, something saw you, sitting there under that hemlock tree. It crept around you in the darkness to get a good position. When it was behind you, it sneaked up - and leaped! And you weren't there, and it hurt itself."

Everyone just stared. "Yeah!" "Sure it did." "Well, that's as good an explanation as any. Let's eat!"

We never did figure out what "it" was - but - whatever it was, it was something I sure won't forget.

Ω

Camping the Comfortable Way

The days are growing noticeably shorter. It's still summer but the nights are cooling off. This is the best time of year for camping out. It's a great time to be in the woods.

Camping can be a pleasurable experience - or it can be a real pain in – well it can be something less than fun. It's all in the preparation, the planning. I don't claim to be the world's foremost authority on camping but let's talk about it a little anyway. You don't have to be Daniel Boone to live comfortably in the woods.

First have a pair of comfortable boots - not "sneakers" but ankle high boots. It's easy to turn an ankle and the boots will give you a bit more support. Wear a good pair of woolen socks - light if the weather's warm. If you're inclined to get blisters, wear a thin pair of nylon socks inside the wool socks. The friction that'd cause a blister will slip-slide, nylon to wool, and not bother your skin. Full length pants and a long sleeve shirt, rugged, to ward off brush and brambles. If it gets too warm, it's easier to pull the shirt off than to wish you had one to put on. You might consider a jacket, too, depending on the weather and a hat with an all-around brim. The hat'll keep the rain or sun off your head and neck and out of your eyes. A little "bug dope" is easy to carry even if you don't use it. Let's be comfortable! This is not a movie - not the place to be "stylish" or "macho," this is the real world.

Oh! And this business of wading through the creek is just for the movies. Keep your feet dry. They're what's gonna carry you back home again.

Have a good compass - and a chart, too, unless you're very familiar with the area. And matches - you might want to wrap some in wax paper or a zip-lock bag in case you fall in a creek. Speaking of a creek, water is an important consideration when picking a campsite. Dry campsites are manageable but you're going to miss wash water. For drinking, bring your own.

Now! What're you gonna eat? Where are you gonna sleep?

There's a lot you can eat in the woods – and some things you shouldn't. But, sure as you count on "living off the land," you won't find anything. Fish are nice but don't count 'em 'til you've got 'em in your pocket. What I do is make up a menu for each meal I plan to have in the woods. List everything - bread and butter, potatoes, eggs, bacon, coffee, (wine maybe?) and right on down the list. List each meal separately and note the quantities. You can combine them later when you assemble/purchase your supplies. How will you cook it? What condomin. . ., condu . ., conundr, - you know - salt and pepper and things like that? List everything! Next, what will you eat it out of - and with what "tools" - and how you intend to clean up? If you cook over an open fire there'll be tar on the cooking utensils. Have you ever tried to clean burned-on pine tar from an aluminum pot or pan? It's a "bear," let me tell you. Carry a couple paper or cloth bags to put these utensils in 'til you get back to civilization. You can cook or heat up several meals without cleaning the outside of those pans – clean the inside, of course, but don't worry about the outside. An added note here: tin plates and cups are either too hot or too cold. Paper plates sound easily disposable – and they are. Just put the dirty ones in the fire. But paper plates are easily spillable too. Melmac or something on that order is my preference.

Each camper should have a good knife. You don't need those machete size things, a pocket knife'll do fine. And a fork and a spoon are handy if you don't want to have to carve one. Divide the load "to each according to his ability." Keep the menus you started with to help you plan and portion out the meals as you create them. There are all sorts of self-heating meals and "add water" deserts and many of them are excellent fare but don't lose sight of the nutritional value of what you select. As far as meals go, a person can live for 30 days or more with nothing at all to eat. You'll need water but nothing to eat. You'll be hungry (for the first day or so, then it kind of fades away). You'll lose weight, maybe even have a headache for a day or so, but you'll survive. But we want to enjoy ourselves so let's don't go that way.

Next let's consider ". . .to sleep - to sleep -

perchance to dream − ah, there's the rub . . ."
Unless you choose a level spot, no rocks or sticks
under you, and a ground cloth or a pad or an air
mattress (and have a pad between you and the air
mattress) you're gonna sleep like that lamb that lays
down with the lion. You may lie there but you're
not gonna get much sleep. Sleeping bags are the
way to go these days - good ones - and, maybe, a
knit cap − we used to call it a "chuke" - to keep your
head warm. Don't scrimp too much on the sleeping
bag. You may save a couple bucks on a bargain bag
at the discount store but you'll pay for it when you
get cold and the padding all wads up on one side.
Top it off with a tent, at least a floored, screened
pup tent. It'll keep out the bugs, let in the breeze,
and keep off the foggy foggy dew.

Well, that's a start. Plan to be comfortable.
On the other hand − if it should befall that you find
yourself in the woods and you're temporarily
disoriented (read that "lost"), the only thing you
have to fear is you, yourself. As I've already said,
you can go a long time without anything to eat.

A little aside here: My father always told me
to carry a little salt. He used to say "You can eat
your own boots if you have a little salt to put on
them."

You do need something to drink though so
always - always have water with you − and matches.
When the woods get dark and you find yourself lost
and alone, the sunny friendly woodland becomes an
uncaring dark forest, a shelter for ominous and

threatening creatures of the night. You'll hear noises out there in the dark – some imagined, some real. Plan ahead. Gather some wood, enough to last the night, and start a fire. A campfire on a dark night can be a real friend and a morale builder. As far as the noises go, there probably are critters rummaging around out there. After all you are in their "house" remember. They may not be overjoyed that you're there, maybe even wish you were somewhere else, but there's nothing out there that's gonna "getcha!" Curl up and get some sleep. Plan what you'll do tomorrow. You may get a little chilly but nothing bad's going to happen. Anyway, with your compass and a chart (or knowledge of the land) and a little preplanning, you've got nothing to worry about. Enjoy the great outdoors!

♎

Come On Along

The Place Where I Worship

The seasons are changing. It's not something that happens suddenly but it's something a person suddenly notices. Winds come more from the north and are stronger. White horses, the white-capped waves on Lake Superior, are galloping in from the deep water. They charge into the rocks and along the shore and explode in geysers of spray. There's a chill in the air even when the thermometer doesn't say so. The wind drags the apparent temperature down a few degrees. You've learned to recognize the message. A northern Michigan winter is just 'round the bend. But in between you know that fall, "Indian summer," that most beautiful time of year is just ahead. It will happen first.

People who study leaves and trees and these things say it's the change in the amount of daylight, the reduced hours of sunshine each day. This triggers some internal system within the trees that cause the circulatory systems to withhold certain vital chemicals causing the leaves to change color and to die. I've then wondered why all the leaves don't change at the same time and rate? I guess that would be explained by some kind of psychology trauma, a leaf neurosis maybe when they were young. Those same people tell us it's that decrease in daylight that causes a male deer to go looking for a female. You might have noticed too that the bucks, the male deer, have grown antlers, horns. I

71

wonder if that's where the expression "horny" originated?

However and whyever the changing color of leaves comes about, they certainly brighten the world. I guess it could be called the golden age of the forest. It certainly lightens the mood of those of us fortunate enough to live here and alert enough to notice.

"Full color" is a will-o-the-wisp expression. If you inquire about it, it either "hasn't yet happened" or "it peaked last week." You learn to just enjoy and not be concerned with the details. I like to think life is a lot like that. We can be so much in a hurry, so concerned about being somewhere or doing something in accordance with some real or imagined "schedule" that we pass up more than we achieve. Life is not a destination. If you think about it, in spite of what all the preachers say, you know what that "destination" is going to be. Life is the journey! Take time to notice the leaves changing color along the away.

While we consider these philosophical reflections, I'd like to share a favorite fall place of mine. It's a good spot to think such thoughts. Some of you may know of it but for those who don't, here's how to get there. From the intersection of County Road 550 north of Marquette and County Road 510 just south of Big Bay, take 510 south. At 1.1 miles on your odometer you'll see a little two-rut side-road on your right. There has been some red "day-glo" paint on a tree trunk there - a sort of a north woods street sign. Wind and weather may have eroded it so watch your odometer and the side of the road. Turn up that two-rut road a half mile. You'll find plenty of room to turn around and park your car. Walk a quarter to half mile farther up that two-rut road and you'll be on a rock outcropping called "Gobbler's Knob." The site overlooks Big Bay, the Huron Mountains, Lake Independence, and Lake Superior. The fall colors blanket the landscape like a huge multi-colored shag carpet. If you can look out over all that beauty and still be analyzing the "hours of daylight" theory, you've got no soul. If you don't think this is one of the most beautiful spots on earth, you'd better go back to your car and go home. You won't enjoy the rest of this trip either.

Back on 510, turn right. The distance from the (original) 510/550 intersection to the Triple A Road is a total of 3.1 miles. You figure out the distance added by the Gobblers Knob detour. Turn right (west) on the Triple A Road. After traveling a total of 7.8 miles you'll be going uphill, almost to the Yellow Dog Plains. At this point you'll be passing through a golden gothic arch, a beautiful natural cathedral. It's nature's gigantic chapel. This is creation – and it's resurrected right before you each year. You can hear angels singing in the sighing of the pine trees and the rustling of the leaves. This is a favorite place.

From here you can either turn around and go back or continue on. If you choose to continue you'll wander through the woods, side roads and byways for another forty miles to the village of L'Anse. You can make the trip with an automobile without any trouble. Do pay attention to your driving. This is a road frequented by logging trucks and the careless may be closer to their God than they realize. Feel free to pull off the road anywhere, stop often and long. It's the journey you're supposed to be enjoying, not the destination.

For the next few miles you'll be traveling through land owned by the Mead Paper Company and witnessing first hand how they "farm" trees to manufacture paper. There are signs along the way explaining it. Seventeen and a quarter miles total into this trip you'll be at a spot called "Anderson's Corner." Turn right onto Ford Road and continue. (Ford road will run into a road called "Northwestern" but you probably won't even notice.)

Stop often, look around, and listen to the quiet. Do stop clear of the road though – the logging trucks – remember? You're apt to see deer, bear, moose, partridge, hawks, eagles, and all the creatures of the forest along this road.

At 28.6 miles you'll cross Big Eric's Bridge and by 29.8 miles you'll be at a stop sign at Skanee Road. Turn left on Skanee road. As you travel along – not too fast now - if you're looking you might see some ripe red apples hanging within easy reach right beside the road. They're not off in some farmer's field, they're right beside the road. Don't

74

be in a hurry. Stop. Try one. They're good. Pull off and investigate whatever attracts you. Remember, you're supposed to be enjoying this trip. After 49 miles (total) you'll be in L'Anse. Turn left at the light and head out of town back toward Marquette.

At the top of the hill at the edge of L'Anse stop at the Hilltop Cafe. You remember my telling you the enjoyment was the trip? Not the destination? I lied! You can enjoy this destination too. They have hot cinnamon rolls fresh out of the oven and big as your head. The butter'll melt on top and – well – it's a suitable ending to a beautiful experience.

Ω

Come On Along

Winter

Winter in our north country is all too often imagined and looked upon as ice and snow and cold, a good time to go to Florida or Arizona or someplace warm. No one is saying winters up here are easy but there are compensations. We have skiing, snowshoeing, hunting, ice skating, ski jumping, snowmobiles, ice fishing, dog sledding – the list goes on.

Another advantage is the changing seasons. There's a reference to compare one time of year to another. Spring is the birth of all things. Summer is soft and easy living. Fall is riotously colorful while winter sees the cessation of life – which is followed by the resurrection of spring. Without all four it's like asking how high is high? In relation to what? You must have all the seasons to compare – and appreciate – one to another.

Hawaii they tell me has a temperature of 70 to 73 degrees every day of the year. Is there anything more bland than that? I have a friend who goes to Florida each winter to a place called "Cockroach Cove." Be honest now. Do you want to come home in the spring and tell friends and neighbors you spent the winter in Cockroach Cove?

♎

Come On Along

A Lantern in the Window

There's nothing so welcome as the sight of a lantern in the window after a nighttime trek through the winter woods

Benny and the North Star

It's December in Michigan's Upper Peninsula. The forest is locked in the icy grip of winter. The birch and aspen and maple stand naked in bright sunlight under azure blue skies. Their bare branches etch distinct shadows on an unbroken mantle of soft white snow. The only sound in this frigid stillness is the muted swish of snowshoes and my labored breathing. Each breath creates a small frosty puff in the cold clear air. My fourteen-year-old son, Ben Jr., follows about three paces behind.

Benny's mother and I are divorced. She lives in Texas with him and his two sisters. I live in Michigan's Upper Peninsula alone. Each hour I get to spend with any of my children is precious.

I have a deep love for the Upper Peninsula of Michigan. Early in life my father introduced me to the great outdoors; the grandeur, the solitude, the silence. Out here alone a person can look into their soul.

The remote cabin we're heading for is sits alone in the northern woods. The cabin was originally built about 1920 – sometime around there. It was later rebuilt after being destroyed by a forest fire, in 1927. The original founder had been a lumberjack and roustabout of the early days. They were the men who could "walk taller, drink deeper, jump higher and fall harder than anyone else - and cut more timber than any other man "in this tin can outfit."'

The great pine forests attracted lumber barons of days gone by. The lumberjacks followed the work. The lumber barons have passed into history but a few lumberjacks are still around. The little cabin found its way through several parties to my father and, when dad died, to me.

The Yellow Dog River flows by just south of camp. The nearest "all seasons" road is about two and a half miles away along a couple of old logging trails. That's the route Benny and I took after leaving our car back near the main road.

When we arrived at the cabin we took off our snowshoes and cleared a spot on the front porch. The key to the padlock on the front door is taken from its hiding place under the eave. The ancient old lock opens easily and the key is immediately returned to the eave. There's nothing of great material value in the little two-room cabin. The lock is to discourage the curious. Anyone in distress could easily enter through a window and their welcome would be equal to their need.

Inside, the cabin is dim and cold and musty. It's used infrequently and its greeting is the same every time. The wood box beside the kitchen stove is full – one of the unwritten laws of the north country. I immediately busy myself getting a fire started in the fireplace. Benny uncovers the windows. The kindling ignites eagerly and the flames begin to eat into the dry hardwood.

The kitchen shelves contain a small stock of foodstuffs; hardtack, coffee, nonperishable things. We have carried in bread, milk, a couple of venison steaks and the trimmings.

The view through the west-facing picture window reveals a forest gripped hard in the death-like embrace of winter. Trees stand stoic and still in the silence. The scene is magnificent in appearance but pitiless toward the unwary or careless. A winter woods is very much like the sea, equal treatment for all but no quarter given.

"Dad, it's only eight degrees on the thermometer on the woodshed."

"How about that? How's the kitchen stove doing?"

The stove lid rattles. "Good! The chimney seems to be drawing all right."

"She'll be warm in here pretty quick." I turn down the blankets on our bunks to let the heat in. No need to be surprised later when jumping from a warm room into a cold-soaked bed.

Benny picks up a water bucket, grabs his coat, and heads for the door. There's a creek out in front of the cabin. He'll have to put on his snowshoes to walk the hundred feet or so to get water. Good lad.

There's evidence that field mice have been in the kitchen. I brush the "evidence" away. A blackened cast iron frying pan hangs on a hook. I remove a stove lid and place the frying pan directly over the flames. Dishes and silverware are taken from the cupboards and placed on the table. When Benny returns with the water, we are on our way to an evening meal that the King of England would envy.

Shadows grow long as the sun moves toward the western hills. The fireplace crackles and dances cheerfully. Outside the outlines of trees and branches fade, blending together. Inside the last delicious morsels of steak and potatoes disappear with hot coffee to wash it down.

Our talk is light and, for my part, somewhat stilted. I want so badly to reach out, to share with my son these things I treasure most. Benny's a somewhat quiet fella, kind of introspective. His momma and I aren't on the friendliest of terms so that doesn't help much. I believe the kindest thing a father can do for his children is to love their mother but that's – well – another subject. I can only offer what I can.

Benny sits quietly staring deep into the fire. I quietly watch him and wonder. What does he see? What's he thinking? Does he feel any communion with shadowy prehistoric ancestors who once huddled in a cave and stared in fascination at those flickering flames? Does he realize those are the same flames that ancestor saw?

The darkness outside deepens. What can I do to reach him? How can I touch my son? We all seem to have lost the ability to openly express tenderness and compassion. We're more conditioned to compete, to attempt to gain advantage, to win no matter what. Ah, but the price we pay for what is quite often only an attempt to protect our egos. A grand lady I knew along life's way once said, "The only thing worse than being vulnerable - is not being vulnerable." But visions seen in campfires are personal things. One enters that realm by invitation only. Quietly I get up and go onto the kitchen.

The yellow flame of a kerosene lamp sheds a golden glow in the darkness. Dish washing and clean up are accomplished without incident. I turn the lamp down low and place it in a south-facing window of the kitchen. The soft light lies gently on the silent snow.

Another log is added to the fireplace. The flames adjust. The birch bark of the fresh log curls and crackles. We again sit silent as shadows flicker and dance on the wall and the ceiling.

A huge golden moon climbs slowly over the eastern horizon. The trees, once more in silhouette, are outlined against the sparkling snow.

"Benny, do you feel up to a hike in the woods?"

Benny abruptly looks up, coming back from wherever he has been. "Tonight? Right now?"

"Yeah. Right now. Look at that moon out there. It's as bright as day."

He's thoughtful as he looks out the window. "OK!"

"You bank the fire a little. We won't be gone long, but it'll be nice to have a warm cabin to come back to."

In the kitchen, I make a thermos of hot chocolate and pack a light lunch to put in my haversack.

Our snowshoes are out on the front porch. Had they been inside, they would have warmed, melted the first snow, frozen, and been practically unusable. A quick check confirms that we each have a compass and some matches. We're ready to go.

The moon is huge and white. The sky is a deep, dark blue. The stars are like diamonds set against a velvet background. I think of my Mother and one of her favorite expressions: "The Heavens reflect the glory of God and the firmament showeth His handiwork."

Benny and I begin by following the track we made coming in, then we turn in a more southerly direction. The moon is just over our left shoulder. After twenty minutes or so I stop for a "breather." Our back trail is the only evidence of life, our frosted breath the only movement. I start out again, still breaking the trail. Benny's turn will come later.

Fifteen minutes go by and the sound of running water is now audible. The Yellow Dog River is just ahead. I turn more westerly and we sight the river where it runs along a gravel bar before turning east. A partially fallen tree leans across the bar and over the river. A shallow windswept hollow behind a log washed up on the bar provides a shelter. We scoop out a sitting area, gather some dead wood and light brush and soon have a small fire crackling enthusiastically.

The river gurgles and swirls as it passes over the gravel bar and around the bend. Deep in the forest somewhere a tree, in the grasp of below zero temperature, cracks with a report like a rifle shot. The sap in its trunk has frozen, expanded, and shatters the trunk.

There's not a breath of wind as we sit by the fire taking in the magnificence around us. We share the hot chocolate and the light lunch, toasting the sandwiches on a forked stick over the fire. There's

not much talk. My Father once did this with me.
There wasn't much talk then either. As the fire dies
down I point out some of the stars in the sky.

"Benny, do you see those stars just to the left
of that tall tree? Over there? The stars that look
like a water dipper? See? The handle pointing
upward and the pan almost on edge?"

We lean close together. Benny has seen the
Big Dipper before. As he sights along my arm it is
just a matter of re-orienting him.

"See that star on the lip of the dipper? That's
Dubhe, a navigational star. We would use it for
navigation back when we were living in Columbus,
when I was flying B-47s across the Atlantic to
England. I have sighted on that star through a
sextant many times."

Benny's not talking much but seems to be
taking it all in.

"There's another star off to the right - see it?
Right over there? See if you can take the distance
between the two bottom stars on the dipper - along
the base of the dipper - and extend that line about
five lengths, you will come to a very bright star.
That star's called Polaris."

Benny is peering skyward and seems to be
following my directions without any trouble.

"Polaris is also called the North Star because
it is always directly over the North Pole. If you can
find that star you will always know which way is
north. Just like the needle of your compass. The
compass will always point to the North Star.

Benny nods his head.

"Here's what I'd like you to do, son: We are at a bend in the river that's directly south of camp. The cabin's about a quarter of a mile away. You break trail from here, follow that star, and lead us back to the cabin. I'll be right with you, but you lead the way. If you get stuck, just ask and I'll help you. Do you want to take a shot at it?"

A couple seconds of silence, then, "Sure."

We put out the fire, pick up our gear, and put on our snowshoes. Benny takes a minute to re-orient himself, locates the North Star, and starts out. The heavens watch passively as we wind our way around deadfalls and brush piles and hummocks of snow.

Benny does well. He twists and turns, but maintains his bearings with the stars, compensating for deviations along the way. We have to angle across the face of a steep ridge but once on top are able to keep a pretty straight course.

Our cabin is in a shallow ravine and won't be visible until we are fairly close. As we top the last shallow ridge the soft light of the kerosene lamp shines through the trees ahead. There is no prettier sight in the world than a soft lamp shining invitingly through a cabin window at the end of a long dark trail.

"Congratulations, Benny, you did an outstanding job!"

The cabin welcomes us in a warm embrace. It doesn't take much to stir up the fire in the fireplace. But it's getting late and eyelids are growing heavy. We fix a cup of coffee and some hot chocolate and stare into the flames and coals of the fireplace. Conversation drags and finally ceases. We yawn and stretch and crawl into our bunks.

Firelight flickers on the ceiling and dances along the walls. Sleep is not long in coming. The fire dies to a bed of coals. Benny, my son, I love you.

♎

Snow Snake

A rare photo of the deadly northern "Snow Snake." It lurks in the winter woods, poised to strike injecting its deadly "Thermal Toxin." Beware ye unprepared!

The Snow Snake

As summer takes leave we transition through fall and winter approaches Michigan's Upper Peninsula. Then, at an uncertain hour, the powers that control arctic air masses and polar ice align their forces in a fateful row. "Troughs" and "pressure ridges" and "millibar readings" combine in ways that arouse meteorologists to quivering heights of "enhanced" anticipation. Then it happens! The wind shifts to the north, down from the arctic wasteland. There's nothing between it and us but a rusty barbed wire fence.

The arctic air picks up moisture over Lake Superior, freezes it, and drives those icy bullets into the lake's southern shore. Thermometers draw back, shrivel right up and disappear. It's the season for long red woolen underwear and to edge up close to the fire. The wind howls 'round the chimney corner like a lost soul. Loose shingles quake and chatter before the frigid blast. A few snowflakes are trapped in an eddy before a sheltered window. They pause momentarily to peek in. Then they're gone, snatched away into the darkness.

Later, as you lie cozy and warm under blankets and quilts, you listen to the storm raging outside. It screams in frustration. You manage a sleepy smile and snuggle deeper into your soft warm cocoon. Gradually the sounds fade, grow distant. You don't recall just when but they seem to disappear completely.

Suddenly it's morning. All is still. The sun sparkles off the clean white snow so bright it hurts your eyes. The scene is beautiful but the outside world is frozen, frigid and rigid and still. Partridge with presence of mind dove headlong into a soft snowdrift and are buried snug under the insulating snow. Rabbits are safe in their burrows. Bear are asleep in their dens. Birds and raccoons and squirrels and all the creatures of the forest have sought out shelter awaiting the storm's passing.

Ah, but there is one creature that stalks the land. When all others have sought relief from the elements it prowls alone and fearless. It's cunning and ruthless and cruel. It is the dreaded snow snake, rarely seen, but its bite can be felt and can sometimes prove fatal.

The cobra of the far eastern nations will rise up in plain sight, inflate its hood, and threaten its victim. Its bite is not swift but it is fatal. The cobra's venom is neurotoxic attacking its victim's nervous system. If not immediately countered with an antidote, bodily systems will fail - shut down. Death follows!

The rattlesnake of the desert southwest in the United States announces its presence with a whirring rattle of its tail. Its strike when provoked is swift. Its venom is hemotoxic, attacking the circulatory system, the blood. Its poisons invade bodily organs causing massive failure - and death. Here too with prompt administration of an antidote, it is possible to save the victim.

The snow snake on the other hand is seldom if ever seen. Its venom is thermo-toxic. It gives no warning, no wavering shadowy hood; neither does it emit a rattling whir. Its advance is slow and insidious. The experienced outdoorsman (or woman) has learned to be aware of its presence. Only the symptoms, as they develop, may alert the unwary victim. To the careless, the unprepared, the incapacitated, it is deadly.

The snow snake ventures forth during the months from November through April and is most active in the severest of conditions. Some have survived its attack through the amputation of toes, a hand, maybe a leg. Others have experienced a sensation as of thousands of needles being driven slowly through their extremities. It's not a pleasant experience and it will be long remembered.

This resident of our northern countries is terribly unforgiving of the foolish, the careless, and the unprepared. It gives no quarter. The key to survival is avoidance. The key to avoidance is preparation, knowledge, and eternal vigilance. Those brave souls who ride the snowmobile trails or snowshoe the backcountry or ski through the wilderness must be aware. This is the domain of the snow snake.

Those who participate in winter sports, snowmobiling especially, are sometimes given to seeking out the conviviality of the many warm and inviting neon-advertised "watering holes" along the way. There seem to be a good number of them along the trails. To those individuals given to celebrating the "designated driver" option is unfortunately not applicable. A "designated thinker" might be much more appropriate.

I believe it's valid to say the younger members of our fraternity seem to feel they are eternal, invincible, able " . . .to fight and never lose." From my vantage point a few years – quite a few years - down the way, believe me when I say that death or crippling incapacity are often only a hairsbreadth away. And the snow snake is omnipresent. If you venture out into the northern winter foolishly or "under the influence," you're inviting BIG trouble. Get a motel room! Sleep under the bar! The snow snake's not going to "getcha" there. Amen!

♎

Come On Along

A Walk in the Night

It had been a beautiful winter day. The sun shone bright and the sky was azure blue. A couple of our kids – 20 plus year old kids - had walked in to our cabin in Michigan's north woods for a visit. It's a mile and a half from road's end to our cabin. There's a snowmobile path I'd made so walking without snowshoes is not overly difficult.

The day passed pleasantly and that evening, relaxing around the fireplace, the talk passed from family matters to recollections of times gone by. Staring into the flickering fire and throbbing coals of the fireplace memories drift in and out of focus. In the gathering darkness the conversation slowed - and ceased. It seemed an ending to a perfect day. But - as so often happens. . .

"We've got to go. School in the morning." Groans and protests - but - that's the way it is.

"You all take the snowmobile. I'll walk out and get it in the morning."

"You sure?"

"I'm sure. Go!" They went.

The sound of the machine had barely died away when Dorothy suddenly said, "Honey, don't you have to go to town tomorrow? Early?"

Aaieeh! She was right! I had forgotten. What to do? Get up extra early - in the dark - and walk out? Or walk out tonight and bring the machine back to the cabin? It was cold out there.

With the sun gone it was getting colder. Well, at least there was no wind that was a plus. I'll go tonight. I dressed warm, put a flashlight in my pocket, and stepped out into more than I had expected.

In the woods nights tend to be dark. There are no streetlights or neighbors whose lights can be seen through a window. Out here the visible world kind of ends at the windowpane. That's how it was when I stepped out the door - black. Maybe walking out tonight wasn't such a good idea. I stood there, resisting the temptation to reach for the flashlight. Gradually my eyes dilated, became accustomed to the dark. The moon was down. The sky was a deep indigo. Stars were everywhere, more than I remembered ever being there. They seemed close, glittering and gleaming in the sub-zero cold.

Through skeletal tree branches against the eastern sky I see the constellation Orion, Orion the Hunter. One of the stars in the "belt" of that group is Betelgeuse ("beetle-juice"). I remember squinting at that star through the lens of a sextant as we flew a B-47 "Stratocruiser" across the Atlantic Ocean. We would "measure" the star's angle above the horizon - its altitude – at a predetermined time to determine our position. I find myself smiling as at an old friend. I wonder if anyone is squinting through a sextant at you right now?

Surprisingly I do not fall on my face while walking along staring at the sky. Peripheral vision is actually better in dim light than normal vision. A person can see "around the edges" better than straight ahead. It has to do with "rods" and "cones" and sensitivity in the structure of the eyeball.

A dark shape rises on my right. It's the upturned root structure of a fallen tree. I recognize it and thereby know where I am. I have often put stale bread on the roots for whatever critters might happen by. The story, written in the snow, indicates that crows are the most frequent diners. If I place the bread out later in the day a fox may come by for a nocturnal snack.

The trail swings north. There's the Big Dipper, standing on its handle, its two lip stars pointing to Polaris, the North Star. My son, Benny, and I followed that star home one night. It's another old friend winking down at me. Thinking about it I seem to have friends everywhere.

Reminiscing as I walk, the trail passes quickly and pleasantly. Familiarity with the trail and the dim starlight keep me right on track. The only sound is the soft squeaky crunch of my boots. Familiar places are all along the route; the mud hole, the cross over, the oaks, the zigzag. Then I'm approaching Nick and Aza Economides' cabin and the parking area - and the snowmobile.

Through the trees I catch a glimpse of an occasional flash of light - an electric light - from a cabin across the river. Civilization is ever encroaching on our wilderness. It gets closer and closer every year. Sometimes I'm glad I'm as old as

I am. I hate to see the "old days" disappear.

The outline of the snowmobile emerges from the shadows, shapeless under its canvas cover. I stow the cover, set the choke, flip the switch to the "on" position, and hit the starter. Suddenly the silence is torn asunder by the bark and snarl of the starting engine. The headlight comes on automatically when the engine starts. The bright light slashes through the darkness stripping trees naked against the silent snow. The soft reflected starlight is gone. The irises of my eyes frantically contract to adapt to this sudden explosion of light. In one roaring flash the delicate structure of starlight and the winter woods is gone. Even the stars seem to draw back and disappear. I sit astride a howling wild-eyed smoke-belching monster. It stares through the night with its single eye, gnashing its gears in its eagerness to spring forward.

A small throttle movement and we leap ahead flashing down a brightly illuminated trail. We are a roaring cocoon of noise and light dashing arrogantly through the silence and the splendor and the stars.

I must have taken thirty or forty minutes walking out. During that walk I was over the Atlantic Ocean, I was feeding the animals, tracking a fox, following the North Star with my son, and reveled in the wonder of the night. It took six or eight minutes to get back to the cabin while blanketed in noise and glaring light. I guess life is that way isn't it? Pretty much what you make it.

♎

Winter Woods

Finding a place to park the car is a problem. I'm on County Road 550 about 15 miles north of Marquette in Michigan's Upper Peninsula. The snow banks are four to six feet high. The road is only two lanes wide. There's no place to park.

About a half mile back there's a side road. A quarter mile in is a house - and a driveway. They're darn nice folks and they allow me to leave my car in their yard.

After thanking them for their kindness I start walking down the road, pack on my back, and snowshoes over my shoulder. The hard packed snow squeaks beneath my feet. When the snow squeaks, the temperature is down. I'm heading for my cabin, the "Natural Elusion," in the woods on the Yellow Dog River. It's easy goin' on the road.

It's nice to have company for a hike in the woods but there are times it's nice to be alone too. A person has time to think, to recharge life's battery pack with no distractions, no noise. The whole aura of the "Natural Elusion" is just such a place.

Beyond the bridge over the Yellow Dog River, the old "Bushy Creek Truck Trail" meanders off in a westerly direction. The truck trail was once a main thoroughfare through this country. It was a stagecoach route from Marquette to L'Anse. It's now a conglomeration of re-routed ruts, old railroad beds, and an occasional side step between a couple trees.

At the start of the Bushy Creek Truck Trail I climb to the top of a snow bank beside the road. The plow-thrown snow is hard. A couple steps beyond and you may sink clear up to your – well, up to your waist or deeper.

It used to be a problem getting snowshoes strapped on, buckles adjusted - and re-adjusted - and re-adjusted again. Now somebody has designed a sort of section-of-inner tube thing that you just slip your foot through and it really does the job. It wasn't I.B.M. or A.T.&T. or Dupont or some computer whiz. It was some guy stumbling through the bushes, just like me, only smart enough to think of a better way.

An empty logging truck passes along the road heading toward Big Bay. The engine snarls and growls while binder chains jingle on the uprights. The rumble fades into the distance and silence returns. I start off into the woods.

In summer it takes about forty minutes to cover the two and a half miles to the cabin. On snowshoes, I plan on at least an hour maybe an hour and a half. The sun is midway down the afternoon sky but time shouldn't be a problem.

The snow sparkles like a million diamonds, so bright it hurts the eyes. The air is cold and still. The naked trees stand stoically still in the cold crisp air, rigid branches outstretched. Evergreens gather their needles around them in solid green relief against the white snow. Everything but time is standing still. Once in the woods, even time seems irrelevant.

The highway is behind me. The quiet of the woods is scarcely broken by the soft swish - swish of each snowshoe step. My breath makes small white clouds. Ice forms on my mustache. I squint against the white intensity.

My small pack is no problem - a half-gallon of milk, a loaf of bread, margarine, a half dozen eggs and a little bacon. There are some supplies at the cabin, coffee, stew, and things like that. My father always kept the cabin stocked, especially in winter. He figured anyone in trouble who stumbled onto the place would be able to warm themselves and find something to eat. It still seems like the thing to do. Maybe that's one of society's problems today? We don't seem to be as concerned with one another as we once were.

A bend in the trail and Bear Lake comes into view. The trail passes through a stand of white birch on the shore of the lake. I've always admired this spot. I stop to catch my breath and look across the lake. It's iced over and covered with snow. Dark pine trees etch the far shoreline, their shadows stretching out across the flat unbroken white snow.

It's quiet - still - nothing moves. No tracks anywhere. No sign of life. I haven't even seen a bird. I feel like an intruder, that I'm desecrating the place with the mere act of leaving tracks. The highway is only a half-mile behind me but the isolation; the feeling of "all alone" is everywhere. A few words of a Robert W. Service poem come to mind:

"The cold fear that follows and finds you.
The silence that bludgeons you dumb."

I could strike out across the lake; pick up the trail on the other side. I consider it for a bit but decide no. It would be sacrilege to deface the soft still field of white that is Bear Lake. Besides I want to see how the narrow neck of land that keeps Bear Lake from emptying into the Yellow Dog River is holding up.

The dark waters of the Yellow Dog cut a black slash through the intense white snow, gurgling and chortling over the rocks, on its way to Lake Independence and Lake Superior. All is well. The bank is holding.

The trail is traveled enough during the summer to keep the brush from choking it. Now, in winter, it's like a paved white highway.

There are many offshoots; skidding trails, sledge trails, some old railroad beds for the "Limey" railroad engines that hauled out the logs. The custom back then was to lay a railroad track into a stand of timber, log it off, pick up the tracks, and lay them down in the next stand. A person can still find an occasional railroad spike along the old grades.

There's a disturbance in the snow ahead. A small "tunnel" pushes up the snow about an inch or so, trails along a few feet and ends in a large hole. There are the outlines of wing feathers on either side of the hole. It would appear that an owl might have dined on a field mouse. It's the first break in the snow blanket I've seen, except for my back trail.

I look back. I'm about two miles from the highway now. If I broke a leg or had some other accident, what are my chances? Hmmm. Lions one, Christians nothing. Nothing else would change. That's part of the attraction, the siren call of the northern woods in winter. You must stand alone - or die.

I continue along the trail past the old apple orchard. It was the site of Logging Camp Five in the old days. A few gnarled apple trees cling defiantly to their tiny patch of earth, standing firm against winter's icy onslaught. Who was it that planted those trees? What were their hopes and aspirations? What finally became of them? Their trees are still here. In the fall, the apples are still good. I wonder.

The trail continues down the cut made by the small creek that flows past Tom "Tin-Can" Sullivan's little cabin. Just past the creek I turn off the main trail on a side road toward that little cabin. Tom used to live up here year 'round. He used to ride in and out on a horse named "Black Diamond." I guess he walked or snowshoed in the winter. It was a lot farther to a road then than it is today.

Tom shot himself in the cabin - oh - about 1928. Too much "all alone," I guess - that and drinking his own homemade moonshine. My father, grandfather, and some other Marquette sportsmen bought the place from Tom's estate and called it the "Yellow Dog Hunting and Fishing Club." Time passed. People moved. Friendships changed. My father and I wound up with the place. Dad died while I was off soldiering with the Air Force and now the place, the "Natural Elusion," is mine, memories and all.

Through the trees I can see the outline of the cabin - straight lines that are foreign to nature. It's the end of the trek. It looks good. My pack straps have begun to feel tight. Shoulder muscles unaccustomed to this use are complaining. The sun is lower and the air is noticeably colder.

The screen door on the cabin is tied open just as I left it for winter. I take off my snowshoes using one of them to scrape the snow away from the door. It isn't difficult. The wind sweeps the porch pretty well.

I open the cabin door. It's dark inside. Some light seeps in around the drawn shades. There's a smoky odor - a little musty too. Everything is just as I left it last fall. There's an old pair of pants hanging behind the Franklin fireplace. I did a little work outside in the fall rain, got them wet, and hung them there. The cabin is like an old friend that's been waiting for me to return.

Inside I start the fires immediately. The firewood boxes are full - one of the unwritten rules of this north country. The cabin seems to sort of stretch and come awake as the place warms up. While the cabin warms I open a trail to the outhouse. There are some chores that just have to be done.

Soon the cabin is warm and comfortable. Supper is heating on the stove (stew! what else?). My favorite rocking chair sits in front of the fireplace. Life just doesn't get any better than this.

The thermometer outside is going down like an elevator. The sun still lights the western horizon and the sky is clear. She's going to be a cold one tonight. There's plenty of wood. The cabin is insulated – well, some insulated - with leaves. Dry leaves are darn good insulation but watch out for fire.

The place has a gentle way of reminding me of what I am: a pretty fragile creature. We humans have developed "tools." We've learned to cooperate with one another to survive. I fear that this is sometimes forgotten in far away prestigious halls of power and affluence. If I forget something here, I may die for it. If they forget something there we may all die. Those folks should be made to spend time each year with the basics, back at their roots, alone, in contemplation. Maybe it would restore a little more honesty and humility to the affairs of our nation.

While mulling over these philosophical thoughts the sun has set. A broad bright moon shines with a blue-white intensity on the snow-covered landscape. Barren trees etch spectral shadows in jet-black relief on the soft white snow. I gaze out the window at the seductive beauty of the environment; so alluring in appearance, so unforgiving of the foolish, the unwary. It's so beautiful, so quiet, so still - so deadly.

The creatures who live there - birds, animals, fish - grapple with these elements continuously, no quarter asked or given. They don't always win but what's even more amazing is that they don't always lose. Natural selection is an efficient but heartless judge.

The flickering flames of the fire reflect in the window calling me back to the "tools" I must use to exist here. I stare at my thoughts in the fire, the throbbing coals. The first of our ancestors to see fire, probably from a lightning-struck tree, saw the same thing I am seeing now. Nothing was different. The basic truths don't change - ever.

My son was once up here with me on a night like this. We snowshoed through the moonlit woods down to the main river. Seated beside a campfire in the snow we heard a tree shatter as the intense cold froze the sap in its veins and split it open. I showed him how to use Polaris, the North Star, to find his way back to the cabin - to a kerosene lantern shining through a window - to warmth - to safety. He's an electrical engineer now, working in the city. I wonder if he remembers that night? I wonder if he'll ever sit up here staring into the fire like this?

This area is building, growing in population. There are more people coming - like lemmings - and we're filling our space. The road in has been improved - part way - with telephones, electricity, they even plow it some in winter. There's a fella' with a dime-store looking pull-behind-a- truck road grader messing around with the trail in the summer. The end of our wilderness may not be far away.

For tonight there's a bed of coals in the fireplace. There's a big knotty chunk to hold the fire. There's more wood handy to feed it during the night. There's kindling and paper to restart it if need be in the morning. Memories drift before my minds eye. Old trails are traveled again. New projects are contemplated. Eyelids grow heavy. The bunk beckons invitingly from the corner.

Under a large puffy quilt I curl up and watch the flickering flames. They dance on the walls and the ceiling. I watch as they tire and withdraw to glowing red coals. Outside the shadows of naked trees move slowly but steadily across the white blanket of snow. Here is peace.

Ω

Come On Along

Ice Volcano
An icy volcano spews forth frigid water in an eruption
along the ring of ice that is Lake Superior's winter
shoreline.

"If Winter Comes . . ."

It's January in the Upper Peninsula of
Michigan. The temperature has been down for
several weeks. The snow seems to have settled in
for the long haul. We went down to Sault Ste Marie
over Christmas. It looks like they got their quota of
snow there - all in one shot.

The guys at the locks are planning to keep the
shipping season open 'til January 15. This first
unexpected snow and cold has given them a real fit
in operating the locks. The ice not only hampers the

opening and closing of the gates but inside the lock itself it doesn't leave room for the ship. The crew often has to partially fill a vacant lock then open the lower gates and help the water wash the ice out. All this takes time - and work - and mumbling under your breath. The ore boats have to wait. They're all trying to make that one last trip.

Driving to and from the Soo we noticed deer tracks near the swamp just east of Newberry. I guess the deer are just now yarding up. Unfortunately there were a few road-kill deer off to the side of the highway. The congregation of hungry crows they attracted made their presence even more apparent. The Department of Natural Resources believes the deer herd is still pretty large in spite of the successful deer season in November. A severe winter could kill off many of them. In the nature of things the road-kill may not be so unfortunate. After all the crows have to eat too.

The swamp area along the Seney stretch looks like a vast white desert. There's enough snow to cover everything under a smooth even blanket. Where the evergreen trees - the pines and the cedar - are thick they tend to hold the snow off the ground. They'll keep it in their branches and allow the wind to blow it on to a more open area. The evergreens do two things actually: they reduce the snow depth underneath allowing the deer an easier time moving around and they provide more accessible browse during the long lean months of winter.

Along the lake shore the ice is starting form,

break up, and to pile up in pressure ridges. Fresh fallen snow will cover these ridges and mask treacherous snow-covered cavities and gaps. These ridges develop and expand outward from shore. If an unwary adventurer strays too far from shore they may fall through one of those hidden gaps. Their chances for survival are not good. They are down in a hole in the frigid water. They're out of sight. And, shouting from down in that icy hole, who's going to hear them?

The coastline of the Pacific Ocean is often called a "ring of fire" because of the volcanic activity around it. Lake Superior's shoreline could well be called the "ring of ice." It, too, has "volcanoes" of a sort. Ridges, domes of frozen snow and ice, form the cavities as we just mentioned. Waves surging in and out trap air in these cavities creating pressure, just like in a volcano.

One day, while I was cautiously venturing along the ice to get a picture, I was darn near panicked by the sudden gigantic sigh of a monster - right beside me. When my heart had slowed to normal again I discovered it was a hole in an ice dome I was on. Every time a wave would roll in it would force the trapped air to be "exhaled" out this blowhole. When the water receded again it would "inhale." If that had been a weaker dome and had collapsed - well - no one might find me 'til spring. Don't go out there. If you must, have a partner watching from a distance. Even then it's not a smart idea. I guess I shouldn't have gone out there either.

Some of those "blow holes" can carry water up and out like a geyser. This surging creates a frigid eruption of water that freezes and builds a mountain of ice – an ice volcano. It's fun to watch but dangerous to go near.

As we pass through Munising there's a tugboat jammed in the ice in Munising Bay. It seems strange that anyone would leave a boat moored out in the bay with winter coming on. There must be a story associated with that. If the laws of physics and freezing water hold true, the hull of that tug will be crushed into nothing but kindling wood come spring.

Aaah, come spring. When January's blizzards no longer howl 'round the door. When the icy wind ceases to whistle down the chimney. Keep thinking spring. Sit close to the stove, keep the wood box full, and stay warm. Nothing is forever. It'll be better come spring.

♎

Spring

Winter doesn't end "all of a sudden," especially in the northern woods. There's a struggle as the sun moves north of the equator, warmth edges north during the day only to be beat back during the evening. But the warmth and the sunshine gain a little more each and every day.

Gradually the icy, deathlike grip of ice and snow is broken. Tiny green shoots emerge in the warm sunlit areas to renew life in and on the earth. Buds, dormant during the winter months, renew their growth. Flowers seem to burst forth, exploding even before all the snow has disappeared.

Long "Vs" of geese are seen. The distant chattering and cackling can be heard as they return to build nests and bring forth young.

Deer appear with newborn fawns. Bear rouse themselves from a long winter sleep and greet the returning sun, often with brand new cubs.

The whole world starts over again, begins anew. A person's spirit, born down by the lengthy gray skies, the cold wind, and the blanket of snow, rises with the return of sunshine, warmth, bird life, and flowering plants. Faith is renewed in the survival of all living things. It's a resurrection!

Ω

Come On Along

Mayflower

A shy spring mayflower rises from the dead leaves of the forest floor. It's a resurrection. It happens in the north woods every spring.

Resurrection!

The sun, moving steadily north, will cross the equator on March 21 (the first day of spring) and continue north 'til it reaches 23° - 27' north latitude. That will be the first day of summer, June 21. During this movement more and more of the sun's energy will be absorbed by the earth rather than reflected. South of the equator just the opposite is happening - they're experiencing fall and the first day of winter on June 21. Isn't it amazing how it all works?

We human beings didn't arrive on earth and arrange all these things, you know. You could even say that "these things" arrived and "arranged" all of us. We were formed, created, designed, and produced by the changing environment all around us - and by our perception of it. Ah, but most of us are too busy grubbing for what we perceive to be our daily bread. We're involved in complaining about the slush and the mud and the traffic, rushing here and rushing there, deeply involved in some seemingly momentous something or other. In the great scheme of things not much of it turns out to be very important at all. Its immediate and overriding importance is that it shapes us. It establishes our references. It determines whether we see the glass as half full or half empty. There's nothing different about the glass − nor about the world we live in. The difference is in the way we see it. If you didn't understand that, go back and read it again. It's important.

Here's something that's too often lost sight of in all these analyses: Life is not a destination - it's a journey. Our modern lifestyle seems to urge us to rush by more pleasure and happiness than we'll find at whatever destination we're hurrying to. A hundred years from now will that "destination" make any difference? in fifty years? twenty-five years? next year? The answer may determine its importance. Whatever you decide it's a good criteria to measure with. Not many of us senior citizens, looking back, wish we had worked harder

116

and spent less time with home and family, for example. As we watch spring approach - and later blend into summer - the remorse is, "so-soon-old-and-so-late-smart." Take the time to watch and to wonder and to marvel at it all.

As spring approaches the power of the sun, "drilling" into south-facing snow banks, rips the white mask away and exposes the sand and dirt underneath. Rivulets of water wash it away and then soak into the earth. Water is so soft but it is also the most powerful force in the world. We can divert it, slow it, delay it, but we can never stop it. All this is happening as life rushes by. Did you ever build one of those road-sided snow-dams when you were a kid? You played at being a "construction engineer" and got your feet wet and caught what-for when you got home. But it was worth it. It was fun! That explains the popularity of the song, "Those were the days, my friend. We thought they'd never end. We thought they'd last forever . . ." remember? You're creating memories now. Don't rush by.

Back to spring. The ducks are here, paired up, and looking for a nesting site. First they'll look in the rivers which are first to have open water. Next they'll explore lakes and ponds. Songbirds return. Goldfinches that have been here all winter are taking on golden summer plumage. Tulips and daffodils poke up through the bare earth on the south-facing sheltered side of the house. The warmth of the sun has heated the earth and they've come alive. In the woods the creeks and rivers are swollen with the newfound life that is the spring run-off.

Trout fishermen lovingly unlimber their fishing rods, oil the reels, get their equipment ready for that "last Saturday in April," the trout season opener. Wildflowers pop up everywhere. If you look close - and are lucky - you may find a trailing arbutus, a mayflower, shyly peaking from under the dead leaves. Look on south-facing hills, warm spots on the forest floor. Get down on your knees, right down near the ground and smell that fragrance. It's worth the effort. That scent, the flower, your enjoyment, it's been hidden in a tiny "seed," a bit of life down there under all the snow and ice. A little smile of sunshine has released this wonder for you and I to enjoy. And it's free! Spring is the time of year that demonstrates, that proves this mystical thing we all want to believe - this thing called resurrection. It's a fresh new start with a clean slate. All sins are forgiven.

The trout fisherman will be in the woods that "last Saturday." Many will have no thought other than the pursuit of the wily brook trout. Me too. It's a relaxing pastime and a noble calling. The wary trout is a daunting challenge and many of us who practice "catch-and-release" fish for the pure pleasure of the sport. Some of my fondest memories are the pauses, the relaxation, toasting a sandwich over an open fire in a sunny wind-sheltered spot. Maybe there'll be a tiny flower - a "spring beauty" - tentatively poking its tiny blossom up from the forest floor. Maybe there'll be a hummock, a hump in the dead leaves. I'd carefully lift the dead leaves away and there'd be the stalk of a fern struggling to find its place in the sun. The "fiddlehead" on that sprout is food - food for you and I too. It tastes a little like asparagus. It's there, all around you, the wonders of creation and evolution. Take the time to look at it. Try a bite of "asparagus."

What's that I hear as I lie back on the riverbank? It's away off in the distance. It sounds like a muted conversation - or a radio playing, volume low and indistinct. No! No, that's not it! Look up! There! There it is! A long, undulating "V" high in the sky. Canada geese are flying north. Watch in silence and listen to the gabbling of the geese. Your heart swells in your chest and you feel all's right with the world. A "feeling" comes over you. "My heart goes where the wild goose goes. . . " We can "radio-collar" and tag them and analyze where they come from and where they go - and when - and how much they weigh - and how long they live. I guess all that is important but I'm not really sure why. Data is fed into analytic machines and facts and formulae derived - but there's no "soul" in all those calculations. It's not the facts but the mystery that makes your heart swell.

Sigurd Olson, a native of Minnesota's Quetico-Superior area, a writer, and an outdoorsman, once said, "Nature is always in equilibrium. It is only when we manipulate it for our own purposes that we contribute to its imbalance." Nature is true and fair - sometimes brutal – but always consistent. And it all starts over, brand new every spring. So can you and I.

♎

Spring in the North Woods

March 21st! That's the day when the sub-point of the sun, the spot directly beneath it, crosses the equator edging northward. The "Vernal Equinox" it's called when spring officially begins.

With the coming of spring the rays of the sun begin to strike the northern latitudes at a steeper angle, less radiation is reflected back into space, more radiation – and heat - stabs into the snow. The snow grudgingly retreats to more sheltered places in hollows, behind banks, in the shadows. As the dark earth replaces the bright snow even more solar heat is absorbed. The snow retreats further. Ice may form in the dark of night but its feeble gain is only temporary. Warm winds begin to pass over the frozen land and into the forests - and so do I.

The water from the melting snow soaks deep into the warming earth replenishing its water supply. The surplus, drop by drop, collects into trickles that become rivulets that form streams emptying into creeks. The creeks overflow their banks and rush to rivers which rise invading the surrounding land producing a wild raging orgy of tangled trees and rolling mud moving irresistibly, on its journey to the sea.

Water! It's one of the most powerful forces in nature. It can be diverted or slowed temporarily. Some of its power can be harnessed but it can never be stopped.

The Bushy Creek Truck Trail up near Big Bay in Michigan's Upper Peninsula follows the Yellow Dog River - approximately. There are parts of the trail, normally five or six feet above the river that may be under water in the spring.

On my way to the "Natural Elusion," my cabin in the woods, I, too, follow the Yellow Dog River - approximately. My four-wheel drive pick-up truck skids and slides throwing mud and water everywhere. I rely partly on memory and partly on openings in the flooded forest to keep me on the truck trail. A little "body-english" doesn't hurt either.

I wonder what spring high water looked like a hundred years ago when old time lumberjacks walked this land? The harnessed spring flood would carry the winter's logs downriver to Lake Independence and on out to Lake Superior. There the logs would be tied into large rafts and towed to sawmills in Marquette or L'Anse.

They didn't rely on the natural runoff alone to move all their logs. They built dams along the length of the river to store up an even larger head of water. Crews would walk the rivers clearing out deadheads (sunken logs), brush, and anything else that might slow the coming log drive. When nature began the spring thaw they had to be ready: store up water, release it and the logs and ride the bucking timber down the raging torrent to the lake.

River drivers, they called them "River Hogs," had to stay with the logs all the way. Any jams or tie-ups had to be released as quickly as possible before the water receded and left the logs high and dry. It was a tricky job sometimes involving standing at the base of a logjam dam and releasing the key log that would collapse everything. The trick, in addition to finding the "key" log or logs, is getting it freed and getting clear without becoming part of the floating debris. Drivers walked the floating logs carrying an eight or ten-foot pike pole and wearing caulked boots - soles with steel spikes sticking out a half-inch or more. Men were killed during these operations and the drive didn't even slow down. It was all considered a part of the job. This was not an amusement park ride.

Some of these "River Hogs" found the caulked boots a useful item in resolving a dispute in the local bars. They knocked their opponent down and "gave 'im the boots." The Marquis of Queensbury was not a lumberjack.

Oh Oh! There's a tree, a large aspen, lying across the road. Aspen are classified as "Hardwood" but they grow rapidly, begin to rot at the heart of the tree, and blow down or splinter off limbs more readily than other trees. This one had had a little help. The stump shows the gouges and chips left by a beaver.

Luckily it's on high ground. I am able to get the chain saw out of the back of my truck and get to the tree without wading.

A few minutes spent examining the lay of the tree can help prevent a serious accident. Cutting a trunk or limb that is under strain can release the tension unexpectedly with catastrophic results. Chain saws are handy and much faster than handsaws I have used but they must be handled with care and respect. The consequence of a mistake with a chain saw can be grim.

Chain saws certainly have made a change in cutting wood - logs or firewood. With the old "buck" saw or the two man crosscut saw, called a "misery whip" by the old timers, it would take a good part of the summer to cut enough firewood to last through the winter.

Damp sweat invites a chill as I finish clearing the road. The truck heater is welcomed.

Everything's high and dry as I pass through the old apple orchard. The trail dips down through a wash. No problem there. I turn off the main trail and stop where a chain blocks passage. The chain has only been there for the past couple years. Twice one year someone had come by the cabin and felt they had a better use for a few things than we did. I don't keep much of value up there. There's no way to prevent someone from breaking in if they really want to. Actually I carry on a tradition my father started of keeping the place stocked with food and dry wood. If someone in real need - lost in the woods, hurt, whatever, (we're a couple and a half miles from the nearest road) found the place it would be there for them. Four-wheel-drive machinery makes it easier to drive the backwoods trails and snowmobiles have reduced the barrier of winter. I keep up the old tradition anyway. If anyone, particularly someone injured with a disabled snowmobile, found the cabin it might make the difference between surviving or not. If you really need it, take it. If you don't really need it, leave it for someone who does.

The police came out to investigate the break in. By reporting it, the police can identify if there is trend. The policeman was a really nice fella.' He made some suggestions. There wasn't much that could prevent theft, but there are a few things that can be done that would help catch the thieves.

There's the cabin just ahead! How many years has it been standing there? Tom "Tin-Can" Sullivan built the place. He settled here, working as a state-salaried trapper. The word was that he used to make a little "moonshine" too; that he developed a taste for his own stuff to the point where he got fired. He took to hunting and trapping for a living; guiding (and providing the game at times) for hunting parties.

Wolves and coyotes were bountied in those days. Now we're bringing wolves in to try to restore a population to the area. The coyotes are still here.

Tom must have been quite a guy. He built the cabin back - whenever. It burned down in a huge forest fire and he built it again. It's been here ever since.

Tom shot wolves and he shot coyotes and he shot deer. He rode through the woods on a horse called "Black Diamond" and would threaten to shoot most anyone who displeased him. The only person he ever shot, as far as I know, was himself. The best the folks who found him could determine he had tried to end it with a rifle, was only partially successful, and finished up with a pistol.

It's hard to know what goes on in the mind of someone living alone far back in the woods - and that many years ago - and drinking some of that booze he used to make. Winters especially must have been pretty hard. Looking back, the wonder isn't that some shacker shot himself but that more of them didn't. No man is an island, Tom. You're not forgotten.

Geeez! The apple trees by the cabin door are swelling with buds. I never noticed that at the orchard back by the river. I didn't notice much of anything except getting in here.

The tulips and daffodils Dorothy planted last fall are poking up. The hyacinths under the window look like they're getting ready to bloom too. Spring is such a - I don't know - a renewing of faith in the possible, a resurrection. The death-like clutch of winter, stark and still and unrelenting, held the land immobile for these many months. Yet, a little warmth releases the land from bondage and the gentle delicate beauty that has always been there appears. It was just awaiting the chance to show itself. The tender shoots quiver in the cooling breeze. You feel you should take it inside - shelter it − but that's not the way. To help it would be to weaken it. We planted it, helped it get started, but now it's got to stand on its own. It would seem there's a lesson in that somewhere.

I'd better keep moving, check the cabin before it gets dark.

There's something about opening the place after a long absence. It's like it's been waiting for me. Nothing has moved. Nothing has changed. The books, the wool socks hanging on a wire over the fireplace, the familiar odors, it's all there. I pause as memories crowd into my thoughts. Enough! Open the blinds. Let the light in. New memories are in the making.

There's a watermark on the ceiling in the kitchen. The old tarpaper roof must have developed a leak. Maybe a torn spot - there hasn't been much damage in here - yet. Maybe a couple of nails came loose? It's funny! Putting the roof on, we drove those nails in with a hammer. A few years pass and they come out by themselves.

I get the fire going. The heat will feel good and the flames in the fireplace will add life to the cabin. I've looked into the world in that fireplace. I've listened to the words of my father, thought of my father as I talked to my son, and wondered if my son was really hearing me. I have questioned myself, watched my children grow, wondered who else might stare into a fire and wonder these thoughts. I've soldiered to some of the far ends of this world, seen luxury to the pinnacle and poverty to the depths – and I wondered about that. The flickering fire provides a perfect atmosphere for speculation and reflection. When the sun has set and the world is still - maybe a coyote yaps up on the hill - I can sit alone and stare into infinity in that fireplace. It brings more questions than answers. There's an inscription on a piece of birch bark on the wall:

"The more I learn, the less I know."

What's it all mean? What's it about? Why are we here?

The fire gradually dies down - and so do I. I didn't get much done today but there's always tomorrow. The bunk has a faint smoky odor. It's a familiar smell, friendly, not offensive. I don't smell it very long.

The morning is chilly. I'm snug and warm under the blankets but I'm going to have to get up eventually. It might as well be now. I throw back the blanket and bare feet hit an icy floor. Brrr!

I wonder what time it is?

The clock shows "3:20." The clock's been showing "3:20" all winter. There are hands on the clock but no numbers. Across the blank face is written, "Who Cares?" There's a message there too.

I didn't prime the water pump last night so I'll have to go down to the creek for a bucket of water.

It's brisk this morning as I venture out in my ragged robe. The sky is pure blue and sunshine is everywhere. It's a beautiful day!

I hear the chortling creek long before I see it. It's out of its banks and tumbling all over itself in its rush to the river. The morning air is too cool for idle contemplation. I dip up a bucket of water and hurry back to the cabin and the fire.

With the fire going and the coffee on a thumping and scuffling from the kitchen startles me. Not so soft as a mouse or so loud as an elephant. I am not alone. I wonder what it is? I pull my other pant leg up and ease on over to the kitchen door. Nothing! All seems quiet and serene. Hmmmm?

Breakfast is uneventful. I go out to the shed for the bucket of roof sealer stored there. Coming out of the shed I'm darn near run over by a brown furry critter the size of a small dog or a large house cat. There's another one in close pursuit. The first one disappears under the shed. The second stops and looks up at me from about four feet away. Then, with only a slight detour, it runs past me and under the shed also. Before I can take another step, out the side come the two fur balls, once fast around the shed and they both stop by the cabin door, about fifteen feet away. I look. They look. Then it's around the field and under the porch. These are a couple ground hogs - in love, from the look of it. So much for the scuffling sounds under the kitchen floor.

It doesn't take much to make the cabin fit and comfortable again. I guess I'm not too fussy. There's evidence that the mice are around. Mice are always around. Trying to get rid of mice in the woods is like railing at raindrops.

When Dorothy comes up here with me there is war! She and the mice are mortal enemies and the battle is without quarter. There's a daily "body count." I try for a sort of truce, a kind of peaceful coexistence between the mice and I.

There's a bird singing out there in the bare branches somewhere. It's just a few notes, but so clear and pure and beautiful. I'm not a birdwatcher but this song is distinct. I thrash through the bushes, binoculars in hand, until I am able to identify it: It's a white-throated sparrow. It's also called a "Canada sparrow." Its song goes "Oh, sweet Can-a-da Can-a-da Can-a-da." So much for bird imitations. I guess it loses something in the translation. It is a pretty sound though.

There are chickadees, too. They're friendly little things. A little patience and a few sunflower seeds and they'll eat right out of your hand.

Geese! First you hear a sound kind of like several people talking at the same time - way far off. Then you recognize what it is. I always hurry out to the clearing beside the cabin to watch the wavering "V" of those Canada geese heading north. It's a sight and sound that never fails to send the blood coursing through my veins.

A whip-poor-will used to come by the cabin evenings just after dark. Its shrill whistle goes on - it seems forever. I haven't seen nor heard it for several years now. I wonder what happened to it?

The wild flowers are coming up in the woods and around the cabin door. I know a few of the names - spring beauty, adders tongue (or trout lily), trailing arbutus, it seems there are hundreds. There are wild strawberry blossoms beside the trail in front of the cabin. The apple trees are in blossom.

Trout season opens soon. The anglers have good access to the Yellow Dog. There's a beaver pond "over the hill a ways" (that's meant to be vague) I know of. As hungry as those brookies are I don't think there are many others who know about it. I'm not going to say any more about it either.

Another coveted secret becomes apparent when the budding leaves get "about the size of a mouse's ear." Morel mushrooms! There are many theories and much discussion about where to look for morels - and when - but, like the weather and economics, nobody knows for sure. Once a patch has been found - well - these are things that wives don't even tell husbands.

I see evidence of deer out by the salt block west of the cabin. Deer are nocturnal creatures and very shy but - as in all things - there seem to be exceptions to the rule. One morning - about ten o'clock - here comes a deer. It doesn't stop at the salt block but wanders toward the cabin. I watch it exploring the edge of the clearing, very casual. I finally open the kitchen door - gently - and ease out. We're now looking at each other across a clearing of about seventy feet. The deer (maybe a hundred pounds or so) looks me over and goes on with its carefree investigation. You'd have thought it was tame. I finally went back inside and got on with whatever I was doing. Darn strange. Haven't had that happen before.

Maybe it senses that I'm not going to shoot it? I've been to a couple wars and kind of lost my taste for shooting things.

There are a pair of chipmunks that live in a large pine stump beside the front porch. Dorothy put a birch bark sign on it:

"The Yellow Dog Hilton"
Chip and Dale - Proprietors

These two chippies start out our re-acquaintance very wary. They run for their stump if I so much as look at them. After a couple weeks we've gotten used to each other. With the sunflower seeds for the bird feeders - some on a flat stump top for Blue jays and nuthatches - the chippies are so busy filling their cheeks with seeds and rushing to and from their stump that soon it's I who have to look out that I'm not run over.

Maybe that's a compliment? From the chipmunks? And from that deer too? Maybe I've been accepted. It's nice to think of it that way. The woodchucks too? Naaah! That was love.

There are several "walkabouts" I take. They're sort of nature trails without the trails part. Over the years a person develops a certain familiarity with the area. The compass can stay in my pocket. Not back in the cabin you understand but in my pocket. "Trust everybody but cut the cards."

I knew an old timer who always said he had never been lost. When pressed by his wife concerning an overnight absence he still claimed to have never been lost but he did admit to having been confused a time or two. I think there are two kinds of woodsmen: those who have been lost - and those who will be.

These walkabouts usually take from an hour or two to an all-day hike. One of my favorites is upstream along the creek in front of the cabin. The creek starts from a number of springs in a swampy area about three-quarters of a mile west. It tumbles down between two rocky hills and flows through the woods past my cabin. After another half mile it empties into the Yellow Dog River.

It's pleasant to listen to the babbling creek in the silence of the forest. I particularly like to find a spot sheltered from the wind with the warm sun shining on it. The creek tumbles by gurgling and babbling at the rocks it passes. I'll find a comfortable seat and watch the forest around me.

Many times it seems nothing is happening. Other times many things are happening but, unless you are very relaxed and observant, you may never be aware of it. By way of explanation: If you've been driving or riding a bus down a street to work - five days a week, 50 or so weeks a year - and. one day, walk down that same street - it's amazing the things you'll see if you just look. A flower growing through a crack in the concrete - a small creek running through a culvert - a bird nest in a tree - a puppy in someone's yard. In life, always take time to smell the flowers.

Today, as I sit quietly listening to the creek, another sound is heard. "Whump - - - whump - - whump - whumpumpumpump!" There's a partridge out there in the mood to attract a lady fair. I listen for a couple of repetitions and then move as quietly as I can toward the sound. Being able to see the bird sitting on a log rewards patience and slow movement. It's back arched, chest puffed up, head erect and wings starting a slow then increasing tempo of beats on its inflated breast: "Whump - - - whump - - whump - whump - whumpumpumpump!" As I tried to move a little closer the bird decided it was time to leave. He departed with the sound of drumming wings. Those partridge! They never seem to get out of low gear.

An old friend, one of the hunters and trappers and wanderers of the woodlands, hasn't been able to see spring in the woods for some time now. He suffered a stroke and he's immobile, confined to bed. He can look at you but he can't talk. He can see. He can hear. I placed a cassette recorder by the creek near the rocks and recorded an hour of "mood music." I gave it to him to listen to. I hope it brings some pleasure. He knows it. He's been there. It's a shame there are so many folks who have never heard it.

♎

Opening the Cabin

Spring is slowly opening the backwoods. The truck trails and paths are no longer closed to all but skis or snowshoes. But I got over eager. I tried to get back to my cabin in the woods of Michigan's Upper Peninsula before the gods of ice and snow had fully relaxed their grip. I got stuck. I had a flat tire. I was up to my you-know-what in slush and slop and mud - and then the jack handle broke. Is somebody up there trying to tell me something?

My little cabin, "The Natural Elusion," has been closed up, empty, since last December. Squirrels live in the insulation in the ceiling. Something has dug under the foundation, made an entrance to the space under the floor. It might be a skunk who has lived there before. Don't wrinkle your nose too quickly. A skunk can be quite a nice neighbor if you don't cross him.

When I arrive the old padlock hesitates, argues a little before it grudgingly releases. The door swings open. The smell is damp, musty. The dim interior seems to come awake, slowly. I just stand in the doorway, looking, remembering. The memories rise up and surround me.

An old telephone hangs on the wall. My grandfather had my father believing that word of my birth (November 15, the first day of deer season, 1929) had been phoned in before dad's arrival with the news. Phoned in? Back in 1929 you couldn't even find this place unless you were lost. The phone was "rigged" - to a battery. It's covered with dust now but it's still there.

A picture on the wall shows a cake I baked in the old wood stove for my son's birthday. Me! Bakin' a cake! How about that? You'll have to ask Benny but I thought it was pretty good.

I don't keep much of value here - don't want to tempt a thief. Not material value, that is. There's a lot here that's precious, irreplaceable, but it can't be stolen. A fella' can get a little teary-eyed just standing here.

Mice! The mice have been everywhere. Dorothy goes right up the wall in her war against mice. Ah, but they've got their place in the order of things too. Almost every carnivorous creature in the wild includes mice in their diet. Mice must have to reproduce at a tremendous rate just to stay even – and they do.

A bed sheet hangs over a large picture window. I remember one deer-hunting season Arvid was looking out that window one night. He hadn't been having any luck and he said that he was going to shoot a deer browsing on apples in the yard.

"No!" shouted Redge, one of our bunch from downstate.

"Yes!" replied Arvid.

Out the door went Redge, holding his pants up with one hand, firing a little .22 pistol in the air, and shouting, "Run, Bambi, run!"

I haven't seen Redge since, gee, I can't remember when. Aaah that man could cook. If he wasn't so ugly I'd have been tempted to ask him to marry me.

It was Tom "Tin-Can" Sullivan who built this place. He was an old timer whose memory is fading in the Big Bay area now. Tom was one of the local character/legends back in the early 1900s. He lived up here by himself. If you crossed him he might threaten to shoot you. I never heard of him actually shooting anyone but he carried a big old pistol. People just weren't that sure that he wouldn't.

A farmer down toward Halfway once penned up Tom's horse, Black Diamond, with some cows that had wandered into his cabbage patch. The guy wanted two dollars a head for the damage to his crop. Tom laid his pistol on the table during the negotiations. The matter was settled without any cash changing hands. He had powers of persuasion, Tom did.

Well, those are the memories - so far - and I haven't even gone inside yet. Maybe we can come up again one day, you and I, and we'll go inside and have a cup of coffee.

♎

Come On Along

A Walk in the Woods

Bob and I had been fishing north of Marquette in Michigan's Upper Peninsula. It had been clear, sun shining, maybe a little cool but an overall enjoyable day. We'd shared sandwiches and a beer in a warm sunny spot beside the Yellow Dog River. Bob had to go back to town that afternoon but I elected to stay overnight at the cabin.

I was up just after sunup for a hot cup of coffee and a stale donut. The mercury had dropped to about 35 degrees that night but, with a clear sky and the sun up, it was warming fast. I started out for what was intended to be a short walk. I was only going to go as far as the beaver dam - but you know how that sometimes goes. Birds were calling to one another, flitting among the trees. They were fairly easy to see - the movement, you know. The leaves weren't out yet and visibility was good. Leaves were coming on fast though, fairly exploding. If I'd have watched closely I believe I could almost have seen them growing.

The water on the beaver pond was a mirror-smooth surface reflecting standing birch tree stubs. The water had risen over their roots when the beaver built the dam - oh, maybe eight or ten years ago. The high water had drowned the trees. I sat down on a slab bench I had built back then to watch the beaver at work. It has held up well over the years.

A couple wood ducks nest here each year. I

139

saw them a week or so ago. I don't see them this morning. That doesn't mean they don't see me though. A red-tail hawk silently wheels high overhead. It circles twice and drifts away down wind. A woodpecker begins to hammer on a dead aspen tree. All seems as it should be. It's so peaceful, so calming and restful just sitting here as a part of this world.

Looking around it would appear that the beaver have moved on. There are no fresh cuttings around the perimeter of the pond. The water is crystal clear. Beaver are mostly nocturnal, working at night. When they've been active, even if they retire to their stick house during the day, the silt they've stirred up will cloud the water for hours after they've left. I wonder if they've gone further up stream looking for a spot where fresh trees and bushes are nearer the water. Maybe I'll go look.

As I cross the dam I catch sight of the woodpecker that's been rat-a-tat tatting on the tree. It's a hairy woodpecker with a little red cap. There's an Indian story that says a woodpecker helped Gitchee Manitou, the Great Spirit, defeat and kill an evil spirit. Manitou rewarded the woodpecker with that little red cap so everyone would know and remember what it had done.

Maybe I'm smarter these days - or maybe it's just that I'm older - but I move more slowly through the woods - stopping frequently. Before the present bait-hide-and-shoot method of taking deer and bear, slow, quiet stalking was a popular way to hunt. It's more of a challenge than sitting in a blind and, I think, and a lot more rewarding. You're stalking the animal in its element and you have to be good - and lucky - to even see them. The animals are, quite naturally, more at home in their woods than we are. Here's a little more wisdom from the Indians. It is said that if a leaf falls in the forest, the hawk and the eagle will see the leaf fall, the deer will hear the leaf fall, and the bear will smell the leaf fall." It takes patience and skill to hunt them - and luck.

During the pauses I notice the multitude of tiny flowers peeking up at me from the forest floor - spring beauties, violets, arbutus (mayflowers). They're all there if you just take the time to look. It helps to know where to look but the flowers don't hide. Trilliums are blossoming rapidly but are not yet as apparent as they will be in a week or so. After a while you get to know the names of some of the flowers but that's not important. They're just as pretty whether you can name them or not.

A fallen birch tree lies across the creek. It looks like the bark has been freshly chewed away. Maybe the beaver have been here recently? There are a series of small dams all along the little stream. These dams are made for the same reason we build freeways: they're lines of communication. Nearly all of the larger predators will kill and eat a beaver if they can catch it. If the beaver can get to water, it's fairly safe - hence the series of small dams. If that beaver is eating birch, he's probably hungry. Aspen and alder bark are much preferred.

A little farther up the creek I turn left and start up a hill. I'm going to climb a rock outcrop that's west of the camp a half-mile or so. I know where there's a bear den up among the rocks. A dead limb lies close at hand. I pick it up, break it off about five feet long, and use it as a staff. The "pauses" come more frequently when climbing that hill. I have to pause and look around a bit too, to orient myself. There was a cluster of dead trees near the den site. They're where a porcupine ate off the bark one winter killing the trees. I'm always amazed, looking at that den entrance that a bear could get into such a narrow break in the rocks. I was there one fall when the bear was "home" so it's residence is not speculation. That time I could smell him. I poked around the entrance a bit - "knocking on the door," you might say. The bear muttered something like, "Woof-ruff-ruff," which I interpreted as; "I am not receiving guests today, thank you just the same."

There are leaves that pretty well cover the entry, no sign of movement, no "smell," so I guess the place is vacant. There's another crevasse, this one horizontal, nearby. Earlier evidence indicated the porcupine probably lived there. No recent signs of life there either. There is a "people" camp visible on the hillside across the valley. There used to be nothing but woods on that hill. Now there's a house. I would guess the animals are saying, "There goes the neighborhood."

Going back down the hill, I cross the creek at

a spot where I once camped for lunch with two of my children. They're both grown now and have children of their own. It was a long time ago but my memory is still strong. I wonder if they remember?

A new, well-worn trail leads alongside the creek. Following it I come upon a snug little one-room log cabin hidden in the woods. This cabin hasn't been here long either. Many years ago I found a rusted pail and a couple of worn horseshoes near here. I would guess there had been a logger's horse shed here a hundred years or so ago.

Cutting over to an old two-track road I met a young lady and her dog. She was heading back toward that little cabin I had just passed - for breakfast, she said. We had a pleasant conversation during which I learned we had mutual friends, a family who lived in a cabin a mile and a half or so away. I also learned that, while I had been fishing the day before, our friends had had a baby boy in that cabin in the woods. A midwife was present for the delivery and mother and son were doing well. So was daddy and I'll see him later today.

Well that's the way life goes. It's the "progress" that's occurring in the woods near my old cabin. As I walk along, meditating over these changes, two deer run past behind me and off into the spring woods. I wonder where they're going? I wonder where I'm going? Maybe we'll get there together one day, those deer and I.

Ω

Come On Along

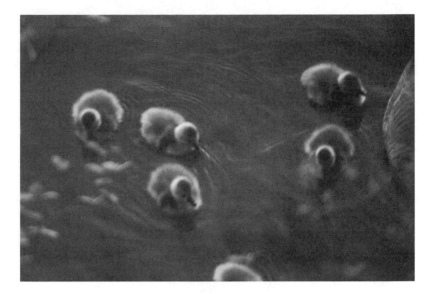

Goslings

These couple day old goslings are learning to search for natural food. These youngsters have a lot to grow in a short summer to join momma and poppa goose southbound this fall.

Where the Wild Goose Goes

It was one of those warm spring days in upper Michigan. I was out tramping through the marsh in front of the house on one of those "honey-do" projects that all you married men are familiar with. It was rubber boots and tough going but, during a brief pause, I overheard a conversation, several people talking at the same time, away off in the distance. I was out in the middle of a cranberry bog and alone. What was going on? Maybe the wind was just right and the conversation was taking place

145

a long way off over - where? Maybe somebody's radio is turned up high? I strained to hear what was being said but I couldn't make it out. I looked toward where the sound seemed to be coming from. Nothing! Then I looked up. And there I saw what it was. Geese!

They must have been a thousand or fifteen hundred feet up, a long wavering "V." One arm of the "V" looked to be a quarter, maybe a half mile long. There were a whole lot of birds up there. They were heading north, going to nesting sites that could be as far north as the Arctic Circle – or a couple of them might stop right here in our marsh.

I had seen sport fishermen in their boats out in the harbor. They were probably after coho salmon or lake trout. Those fish follow the smelt into the shallow water every spring. The fishermen follow the fish. That's a sure sign of spring.

The smelt seem to have faded considerably from the spring "smelt runs" we used to know in "the good old days." We used to line the riverbanks, waiting. Someone would start a fire. It would get dark, and cold. Somebody would have brought some beer - and maybe a jug of "Old Cordwood" - to ward off the chill, you understand. Then somebody'd holler, "They're runnin'!" We'd all rush to the riverbank and dip our nets to beat the band. Nothing! Then the cry would go up, "Who's the (bleep) who hollered 'they're runnin'?" There would be accusations and good-natured arguments by the fire as the jug was passed around. Then, like as not, someone else would holler, "They're runnin'!" We took the bait every time - and that meant it was spring. And the early flowers and the grass turning green, it all meant spring. But when those Canada honkers fly over in their wavering formation, cackling and chuckling to one another, changing the lead now and then, it's then that I pause in whatever I'm doing and I watch. That's really spring. And it's all those thoughts, those memories of the "long undulating line," memories that stretch back over the years. That's the reality of spring up north. Everything old is new again.

That "V" formation the geese fly didn't happen by accident. There's a thing called "wing tip vortices." It's created by the swirl of high(er) pressure air below a wing, off the tip, and curling up into the low(er) pressure area above the wing. This swirl of air broadens and continues behind the wing. The updraft that's created is utilized by the following bird(s) as an aid to their flight. That may be why the lead of the formation changes from time to time, to give the leader a break. Leadership of the flight is not, as was once believed, a wise old gander but more often a wise old goose, a female.

The Canada goose tends to pick up a bad reputation around people. The goose is known to "eat when it's hungry, drink when it's dry, sleep when it's sleepy, and . . ." well, it leaves its calling card wherever and whenever the urge occurs. As a result people sometimes find that the joys of going barefoot in the park may not be all that joyful.

Ducks are philanderers, you know. A mallard duck will chase from one pretty little thing to another. The Canada goose, on the other hand, mates once and is faithful for life. There are cases where a healthy goose chooses to remain with a disabled mate rather than migrating south. I would guess there are human spouses around who wouldn't mind their partners acting more like those geese. While walking in the park however, and after you've just "stepped in it," it's difficult to concentrate on those magnanimous thoughts.

Geese are territorial too. They respect each others "space," and nest early. The goose will lay five or six eggs and incubate them (25-28 days). The gander will stand guard close by. They'll both defend their young against any and all comers, together or singly - including you and me.

Turtles - the bigger turtles - are a constant threat to the goslings. While the young are small and unable to fly, turtles may attack them from under water, grabbing their foot and dragging them down and away from the adults. Not a pleasant thought but one of the realities of life. Large pike have been known to dine on a young gosling too.

The goose family will stay together for a year or so. Each fall there's you and I, the hunters, to contend with. But geese are prolific - brave, courageous, bold - and prolific. There are many things to admire about them. Remember that next time you're "barefoot in the park" and "step in it."

Ω

Summer

Having four distinct seasons is like having salt at life's great banquet table. Fall has to be the most beautiful. It equates to a person's "golden years." These are followed by the cold white stillness of winter, the death of living things. Then comes the resurrection of spring and the relaxation of summer, when "the livin' comes easy." The sun is warm, the breeze is soft, the rain is gentle, and life is good.

Success has many definitions. Those who feel "he who dies with the most toys wins" qualify as having some sort of mental illness. Being able to make a comfortable living while doing the thing you enjoy is my personal definition. It's easy to be sucked in to the "rat race" of material possessions but the price a person pays is their soul. There's a lot to be said for liking "old dogs and children and watermelon wine." Summer is the time to find a quiet place and examine where your life is going – and if you want to go there.

Summer is the time for all living things to mature. It's youth and middle age together. Youth is in a rush to – somewhere? Middle age fears they have passed it. Fall is the realization of what life was about: old dogs, children, and watermelon wine.

Ω

Come On Along

Fishing the Yellow Dog River

Nicholas Elmore, visiting from Fort Worth, Texas, gets some instruction on the important things in life from his Grandpa.

Summer on the Yellow Dog River

It was a dirt road northwest of Marquette in Michigan's Upper Peninsula, old County Road 510 running south from Big Bay. The weather has been hot and dry. Dust swirls behind my pickup truck as I drive south. There isn't usually much traffic along this road but a car has just passed. I was chewing on their dust. I could taste it. It was grinding between my teeth. The boards of the Yellow Dog River bridge rattled beneath the wheels as I crossed. I caught a brief glimpse of water tumbling down among the rocks. It looked cool and inviting. Cool. At a wide spot in the road - good visibility both

151

ways - I jinked back and forth and turned around.

There's a turn off, a parking area on the south side of the bridge. I parked clear of the road and walked over to look down at the water. The river water was very low. We'd had no rain in quite a while. The taste of dust was still grinding between my teeth. I didn't seem to be able to spit it out. Golly but that cool water looked inviting.

Have you ever impulsively stripped down and jumped into a cold, flowing stream? just on the spur of the moment? Ah, that first cold is a shock but later it's not so bad. I glanced up and down the road, weighed the probabilities, and reached for the buttons on my shirt. Just then a car came billowing around the corner, dust curling up behind it. Yeah! So much for any privacy. I waved as it passed. The couple in the car waved back. They must have been local people. Folks from the city don't seem inclined to wave at other folks - something to do with getting mugged, I suspect.

That passing car kind of put the quieetuss on a sudden dip right then and there. Staring down at the chortling water the temptation was great. I began reviewing where I was going, and why, and if there was any hurry to get there. This was not some vast, profound, cosmic-look-at-life. It was more like what time is supper tonight and do I have anything important to do before then. The answer to that question - the water splashed and bubbled – that question was - it looked so cool and refreshing. The question is - - maybe there's a couple brook trout in that quiet pool down there? It looks like there ought to be. The - the answer - to - - what was the question again?

There's a side road - a two-rut trail back up the road about a quarter mile. It runs west along the river. It didn't take much longer than our talking about it before I was heading west along that trail.

This old road is a whole lot better than I remember. It's been getting a lot more use from the look of it. There are a lot of tracks and the vegetation - grass and weeds - is gone, worn down. Golly, there's a cabin over there. I don't remember that. It must be new. And there's a sign; "No Trespassing." Geeez! Those signs are popping up everywhere. It's getting so a fella' - - and there's another cabin, a nice one and looking pretty recent. Pollution! That's what it is! People pollution! This road used to be four-wheel-drive country. Now a person could drive a Cadillac through here.

Passing close to the river now and again I select a spot where I can pull off clear of the road. The woods pretty well shut out any wind and the bright sun shining from a clear blue sky is hot, baking everything not protected by shade. Even the shade isn't cool. As I eye the river, anticipating a cool dip, two guys come walking along the road wearing waders, fishing poles in hand.

"Any luck?"

A shake of the head.

"Nice weather."

"Yeah, but hot!"

I nodded. So much for skinny-dippin'.

My fishing pole and boots are always in my truck. It didn't take but a couple minutes and I was in the river wafting a fly onto a riffle on a quiet pool. After two or three attempts and no action I added a bit of trailing red "survey" tape to the lure - just a small piece. It was more to let me track the lure than with any hope of enticing a strike. Drifting my red-tail fly along the bank I did attract a little trout - three, maybe four inches long. The fish casually drifted out from under the overhanging bank, disdainfully inspected my offering, and idly rode the current back into the shadows. I think that fish was telling me something.

Back on the bank, I sat on a log and watched the stream roll by. Small shrubs, even those on the river bank, had leaves curling in on themselves. Dry! The ground is too dry. We need rain badly.

The temptations rise to strip down and jump in. The passing water chuckles at my idea. Yeah, but someone else might come along - some women maybe. I guess I could grab an oak leaf from somewhere in an emergency. Yes, but walking on those river-rocks is not as "gay and carefree" as the movies would have you believe. No, I think I'll just sit here and enjoy the sunshine, the blue sky, the quiet woods, and the laughing water. There's no hurry. It's true, what they say you know. A bad day fishing is better than a good day at work.

Ω

Stranger in the Night

It had been a beautiful blue sky, sunfilled day in the woods of upper Michigan. It was one of those days when it was sweet pleasure just to be alive. My only concern in life at this particular moment was an old beaver dam on the small creek just up from my cabin. The dam hadn't been occupied in several years and a large hole was letting all the water escape. I had been wondering if there wasn't something I might be able to do to set things back as they were. If I could manage even a partial repair, encourage a few trout to take up residence; maybe a passing beaver family would recognize the potential of the old place. There were plenty of aspen and a lot of alder brush around and even an old mound of earth and sticks that had been a beaver lodge at one time. My own cabin was far enough away that I didn't spoil the neighborhood. It had possibilities.

The better part of the afternoon was spent poking and prodding around attempting to put together some sort of plan. Finally I just stretched out under an aspen tree on the bank to consider what information I had gathered and listen to the soothing music of the gurgling creek. The sun was a warm presence sparkling through the leaves and dancing on what water remained. Casually chewing on a stem of grass, I laid my head back on the soft moss and thought how fortunate I was to be able to experience all this. The creek flowed, the sun moved, and all was well with the world. This was a typical "hard day" at my office.

Hunger finally coaxed me to get up and walk back the short distance to the cabin. I had left a pot of stew simmering on the back of the wood stove. Hot stew! There's nothing like a bowl of hot stew when a person's hungry, with a little wine, of course. We must retain some degree of civilization. But the best sauce in the world - hunger, would top off the meal! With everything set up, I ate slowly, savoring each bite. The sun sinks slowly toward the hills in the west. Shadows grow longer and darkness oozes up, gathering and thickening in the low, shaded areas. A crackling fire in the fire-place keeps the approaching chill of the evening at bay. All is right with this little world.

Clean up is not a problem; a splash of water, a swipe with a cloth, and a quick rinse from a boiling kettle. I have the latest in "drip-dry" dishes and silverware. The darkness of night gradually rises from the hollows and takes over the forest. The dying light of a fading sun still silhouettes a few of the taller trees. Soon they, too, will blend into the darkness that will rule until the moon rises. Leaning back in a comfortable old overstuffed chair in front of the fire I watch the pattern of the flames as they slowly consume a maple log. A person's mind can wander through infinity while watching a fire. Who was it that watched that first fire? It had probably been started by a lightning strike. Fire is one of the constant, unchanging things from that first day so long ago until now. What I'm seeing is what that ancient predecessor saw so long ago. I wonder what they were thinking?

Eyelids grow heavy under the weight of such profound thought. A comfortable bunk beckons from the corner. A yawn and a stretch and shuck the clothing and the cares of the day. I'm soon burrowed under a warm blanket casually watching firelight flicker and dance across the ceiling and along the walls. The first person . . . flickering . . . walls of a cave . . . thought . . .

Suddenly - - why am I awake? The room is totally dark. Coals still glow in the fireplace but inky darkness is everywhere else. Looking across the room at the window I can see a nearly full moon bathing the area in a silvery light.

Then there's a noise! It sounds like silverware sliding around on the drain board - "drip-dry," remember? That must have been what woke me. Maybe it's a mouse. There was evidence of mice when I first arrived but then again there's always "evidence of mice."

There it is again! Whatever it is, it's in the kitchen. I wonder what it's doing in there?

The outline of the kitchen doorway shows dimly but the kitchen is dark. I have a flashlight beside the bed - one of those six-volt sealed-beam types. What to do? I could get up and chase the mouse around the kitchen in the dark. That prospect doesn't make my heart pound. It's been quiet for a while now. Maybe my little friend has found whatever it was looking for and has left. If he's happy, so am I. I'll think about it again in the morning.

Suddenly there's a much louder clashing and clattering. That mouse must be moving the trash can around. I've got to see a mouse that has muscle like that. Slowly, quietly, I slide out from under the blankets. Oooo! That floor is cold on the bare feet. I reach down in the darkness and find the handle of the flashlight. I pick it up and gradually ease my weight off of the bed. No noise. No squeaking of springs. The kitchen is quiet again too.

I slowly feel my way the short distance to the kitchen doorway. I am now able to distinguish shapes in the dim light. All is quiet.

My plan is to ease myself into the kitchen doorway - no sudden movement. I assume that mouse can see in the darkness much better than I. If he senses my presence he will be gone. If I can fool him, remain motionless in the doorway while I pinpoint his position by any noise he might make, then, by carefully aiming the flashlight, a quick push of the "on" button, and I should have a well-lit look at "Super mouse."

I'm in the doorway now, every sense straining - listening - staring hard into the darkness.

Nothing!

Maybe he's gone? Wait. Patience.

There it is! A noise like a zipper! Loud! It's

to the left, by the refrigerator.

From my position I'm unable to look toward the source of the sound. There's a brick chimney on my immediate left with the kitchen stove backed up to it. The wood box is next, between the stove and the refrigerator. The refrigerator is against the far wall in the corner. Two square windows are adjacent to the refrigerator on that far wall, with a small table just below them. What's on that table that would make a sound like a zipper?

"Zzzzi- i- i-pppp!" again.

Slowly. Quietly. I ease forward, raising the flashlight, aligning it. As I clear the raised back of the kitchen stove I am able to see the outline of the open windows and the moonlight beyond. The woods and trees are visible - and moonlight - and - and - - THERE'S SOMEONE LOOKING BACK AT ME!

Everything stops! Nothing moves. My heart is banging against my ribs and my throat is constricted. Is someone there? I'm looking again – hard – and I don't see anything, just the window, the moonlight, and the woods beyond. There's nothing there!

Was someone there? Nothing! Silence! The mouse! Was there a mouse? Something was making that noise – what was it? What do I do now? If there was nothing, that's fine, but how will I know? Something must have been there. Was it my imagination that saw someone looking back at me? How do I find out? Well, I guess I could go over to the window and look.

The spell seems to be broken as I move, around the corner of the stove. The sound of my heart beating seems to shake the walls of the cabin. I try to control my breathing - almost strangling myself.

Slowly, ever so slowly, I lean over the table and peer out the window. All is calm and quiet and peaceful and still. There's nothing there but the moonlight.

Use logic! Let's be logical now. I'm away out in the woods, a couple miles from the nearest road, and there are no neighbors. Who would be wandering around in the woods at this hour? There was a mouse in the kitchen. It probably heard you and ran away. You, trying so hard to see in the dark, looked toward the window and thought you saw someone standing there – and you scared yourself. I think that's how it was. But was someone really there? - or was it just the shadows? There'll be no sleep 'til I solve this thing. Better look around a little more.

I ease along the table, away from the refrigerator and toward the sink. There's another window around the break in the wall and over the sink. From there I can get a good look in that direction. There's a clearing out there - and a trash pit - back away from the cabin.

The indifferent moon silently bathes the area in soft light. Nothing is moving. Relax now! If I look too hard the trees and stumps will start moving around - not when I'm looking, of course, but I'll see them move out of the corner of my eye. My breathing is a bit more regular now. My heart has settled back into my chest.

It's a beautiful night. Peaceful. Quiet. Moonlight. And all seems well with - WHAT? It's right there, not three feet away under the window. It's looking up at me. It's big and black and right there in front of me! It's a BEAR!

Nothing moves. I don't even breath. I don't blink. That bear knows I'm here. And I know he's there. What's next?

The bear casually looks off toward the east. I'm guessing it weighs about 200 or 250 pounds. It must have smelled that stew I had for supper. The bear looks back at me. Time passes – maybe three days. Casually the bear swings its head to the right, then ponderously turns and ambles across the clearing about twenty or thirty feet. It stops again and looks back toward the cabin.

My courage has increased by the square of its distance from me. I reason that the bear is in perfect control of his destiny. It smelled the stew, considered complications, the confusion, and this wide-eyed, irregular breathing, heart thumping creature peering out the window. The conclusion seems to be, "Who needs it?"

I raise the flashlight, aim it, and press the button. The bear just looks. I take a deep breath and make a loud noise. (Well, to me it was loud.) The bear turned and kind of galloped over the hill into the woods - not fast - but it did run.

Before going back to bed, I put the kitchen windows back in their frames. I don't think there's much chance that bear will be back tonight. If it does come back – that was very good stew - with an urge to come into the cabin, there's not a whole lot I can do. I have a .22 rifle but I might as well go after him with a cedar switch. It that bear comes back, I'll "share." When it comes in, I'll go out. That seems fair.

Fortunately the "vendetta" type thinking that warps the human brain doesn't motivate animals. That bear wasn't the least bit offended. I'm not important enough in its life to care about one way or the other. I'm not offended either - scared maybe, but not offended. Armed with all this logical thought and intellectual analysis I crawl back into bed. I don't leave the door open and, believe it or not, I did get some sleep.

The next morning the evidence shows that the bear had been raking the window screen with its claws. That screen must have been confusing to it. If it had been serious about entering through the window, the screen would have lasted about as long as dust in a windstorm. Ah, well, best to get the "what ifs" out of my mind.

Through the following weeks crushed ferns and disturbed vegetation showed that my neighbor, the stranger in the night, was still around. Actually this is the bear's neighborhood and I'm the stranger. Looking at it that way, the bear is allowing me to live here. He is tolerating me. The least I can do is return the favor.

I hope a hunter doesn't get him. I'm not anti-hunting but I've been to a couple wars and have had enough of the killing business. It's nice to have the animals around as neighbors. It would be nice if we didn't surprise one another in the dark of night though.

♎

Come On Along

The Woods in Summer

" . . . and the livin' comes easy."

A soft breeze sighs through the trees, boughs lazily lean with the gentle wind, leaves stir sleepily as their rest is disturbed. Dappled spots of sunshine dance on the forest floor. A small brook chatters busily on its way to the Yellow Dog River. The grass is soft on my back. I peek through half shut eyes from beneath the brim of my hat. The sun is warm.

I watch an ant crawl energetically up a tall stem of grass, move left, then right, its antenna waving in the air. Getting its bearings (or not?) it quickly descends to earth and appears to wander left and right and circles over its own track. It reminds me of an expression a navigator might use to get a pilot off his neck: "I don't know where we're going but we're makin' good time."

Good luck, little fella.

It's decision time. I'm living alone in the woods of Michigan's Upper Peninsula, a couple miles from the nearest road. It's summer and life is easy. Should I get up? or not? I think I'll lay here a bit and consider the situation. One shouldn't make important decisions in haste.

A few years ago I had the option of continuing to work - I was only in my forties - or, by budgeting pretty close, becoming a gentleman of leisure, a philosopher, a bum. I had put 20 years in the United States Air Force, had several pilot ratings, and an opportunity to fly for an airline. I had done some corporate flying, air ambulance work, sales, airport management. I came to a decision almost unconsciously. As a result, it doesn't appear I will ever be concerned with the heavy responsibility that accompanies great wealth. I don't think I will ever be troubled with ulcers either. If you would care to talk of fishing, sailing, flying, roaming the forests, the mountains, the deserts, the seas, I'm your man. I believe God has smiled on me for reasons of which I know not. Thank you God, especially for days like today.

Upper Michigan doesn't enjoy many days as perfect as this one. We - well, many of us - have learned to appreciate them while they're here.

"Nine months of winter and three months of tough sledding." Ahh, but those three months are great if you forget about the sled (It's really longer than that.) One of the local stories tells of a logger who would whitewash the skidding trails in the spring to fool the horses into thinking the trails were still ice. They would continue skidding logs right up 'til summer.

Some years the mosquitoes are worse than others. I don't know what determines that. It seems they're either very scarce or they're everywhere. When the dragonflies are flitting about in the sunny areas, the mosquitoes are gone. In the shade, where the dragonflies are absent, the familiar whine of that little high-pitched mosquito engine puts your total system on alert. It's not really the whine that's the problem, it's when the whine stops. Who of you hasn't lain under the blankets of an evening and listened to that sound grow - - and diminish - and pause - - and whine to life again - - and stop! That's when all senses go to red alert. Some folks wave aimlessly during the attack, hoping the creature will be discouraged. Heh, heh, heh. She never is. Others rely on immobility - pretend there's no one there. It seems that infrared mosquito sensors know otherwise. Just wait! All senses rose to maximum intensity. You know she's coming (it's the female who gets you, you know), you just don't know where. Then you feel her! She's landed on your upper lip! She's about to plunge her proboscis into your tender skin, injecting an anticoagulating fluid that will allow her to fill up on your blood and leave you with a powerful itch in a very inconvenient spot. Quickly now! Tear your arm from under the covers; swiftly deliver a fatal crushing blow of massive retaliation against this unprovoked attack.

You succeed in belting yourself right in the nose. Then - silence! Listen! There's that whine again. Skill and cunning (hers) has overcome ignorance and massive retaliation (yours).

Make friends with dragonflies and birds. They know how to handle the problem. We make much ado about our interceptors and missiles and their ability to attack targets while self-guided. Swallows and dragonflies have been attacking mosquitoes that way for thousands of years.

The "Cat Skinners," those loggers who drive the tractors, would bend the engine exhaust pipes to direct the exhaust right at themselves. The exhaust kept the mosquitoes away. That exhaust is poisonous stuff - carbon monoxide. No one kept records on what it did to the drivers. I hang a couple of those "No Pest" strips in the cabin and put on bug dope when I go outside - "chemical warfare."

I guess I'll get up. It's about time to hike out to the county road and see if there's anything in my mailbox. It's been a couple days since last I looked. Ed McMahon writes to me occasionally telling me that I may "already be a millionaire" in whatever that contest is. Oh, well, I guess that's better than no mail at all - or bills. There aren't many bills though. When you live in the bush you don't need much, you don't buy much - so - no bills. Maybe I should go into politics? I think they need that approach in our nation's capitol.

I have, on occasion, gone in a straight line, cabin to mailbox, following a compass. It's a little more difficult in some spots than following the trail but it adds some variety to the mail run.

The area north of the US41/M28 highway between Marquette and L'Anse is pretty much the way God made it and the loggers left it. There are few fences or roads or property line markers there.

My mailbox is about two miles going straight through the woods. Once, while dodging low branches skirting swampy spots and climbing hills, I came upon one of those 8 x 10 signs, "NO TRESPASSING," tacked on the trunk of a tree. I don't want to violate anyone's privacy. Private property is a thing to be respected but, come on, we're in the middle of the woods. I'm probably the only one who's been here since the sign was put up. I'm not even sure exactly where I am. The next person who sees it will probably be lost.

Small parcels of real estate are often sold to people from a big city or other hostile area who feel a need to protect what they feel is theirs. My feelings aside, I'll readily stay off the property but tell me where it is?

The Yellow Dog River is a well-known trout stream and the paths along the bank bear witness to its popularity. Some folks do well and others don't: there are fishermen and then there are fishermen. My grandfather instructed me at some length, many years ago, about the wariness of the trout in avoiding the angler's hook. He was a believer in a "government pole." That's an alder branch cut near the bank of the stream with a string and hook tied to the end. He recommended creeping to a likely fishing hole on hands and knees or even crawling on your belly. Don't jar or shake the earth. The fish will sense this. Carefully place the bait in the stream and catch the fish by surprise - literally.

I felt his approach was kind of radical. Besides, a fella feels downright foolish if someone walks up on him crawling on the ground with a stick in his hand. It'd be embarrassing!

I had occasion to be up in the mountains in California one time. I was attending one of those military survival schools. Eight of us had been in the bush for a week and we were darned hungry. A hook and a line came in the survival kit they gave us. I caught a grasshopper, cut a "government pole," and slid up to a little creek on my belly like a reptile. We ate fish that night thanks to my grandfather.

There is no mail. Oh well, it was a nice day for a walk. And I needed the exercise.

Returning to the cabin by way of the Bushy Creek Truck Trail I stop in a beautiful stand of white birch trees overlooking Bear Lake. Bear Lake is entirely spring fed with a small creek overflowing into the Yellow Dog River. By the end of July or the beginning of August the water in Bear Lake has warmed up some. I have cached a bar of soap under a piece of bark in an old stump near the shoreline. Today, warm, with the sun shining kindly from a clear blue sky, it seems like a perfect time to take a bath. There's no one on the lake. Now and then there may be a boat or canoe with a fisherman or two. The walk has been warm and raised a little perspiration. The water will feel good.

I strip off my clothes and hang them on a limb, collect the soap, and ease my naked body into the water. It's a little cool at first but the body soon acclimates to the temperature. After washing and re-hiding the soap, I swim out from the shore, float on my back and just relax. The water is cool. The sky is blue. The pine trees sway ever so slightly in the gentle breeze. The sun sparkles on the water like acres of diamonds. Where is life any better than this? I've been told that Heaven is a wonderful place. No offense, Mr. Preacher, but I'm not real anxious to leave here. The area's building up though. With all these people moving in – well – we'll cross that creek when we get to it.

The sun moves across the sky toward the hills to the west. Dragonflies stay around long enough to let me wind-dry and get dressed without mosquitoes.

Thimbleberry bushes have spread their broad leaves on both sides of the trail. Their blossoms are everywhere promising a good crop of berries. If you've never had thimbleberry jam on a hot piece of toast, your life is not complete. The berries don't have a long shelf life. When they're picked you've got do something with them quickly - jam or on cereal or just eat them.

There are raspberry bushes just around the bend in a clearing that was once a small garden. They have gone wild and form an almost impenetrable thicket. There are blackberries near my cabin. Wild strawberries and blueberries, too, seem to grow well there. The flavor of these wild berries is something that just isn't there in the domesticated bushes. I like them all but those that grow in the wild are special. The other creatures of the woods like those berries too. One has to learn to share: if a bear is there, it's his share.

Earlier this summer a black bear wandered by the cabin. I was able to get a picture of it investigating a log beside the path to the outhouse. The bear is gone but the picture causes my wife, Dorothy, great concern whenever the outhouse enters her plans.

We see paths through the ferns and bracken occasionally where "our bear" has passed. We don't bother him and he doesn't bother us. The arrangement seems to work well for all concerned. There's a crevasse in the rock up on the hill west of the cabin. My brother-in-law, Don Salo, discovered it one fall. A bear had been dragging brush into it and making the place home for the winter. It's nice to have him as a neighbor - the bear that is. The view from the rock just above that bear's den is spectacular. Our cabin is hidden by foliage but the rolling hills, rock protrusions, and Lake Superior visible on the northeastern horizon make the climb worthwhile. It's a good place to watch clouds. A person should do that every now and again – watch clouds.

I found a columbine, a beautiful flower, up there, struggling for survival in a crack in the rock. I dug it up, wrapped the roots in my handkerchief, and carried it back to the cabin. It's planted under one of the windows. It's been coming up every year since. Every time I look at it it tells me of the walk about when I found it.

The Yellow Dog River slides silently through the forest, chuckling occasionally over a rock, wandering casually this way and that. I swim in the river occasionally but let me tell you it's chilly. I remember hearing about a forest fire - oh - back in the 1920s - when several lumberjacks and a team of horses spent four or five hours in the river. The forest was ablaze all around them and the river was their only choice. I guess you could say they were between fire and ice.

The evidence of the old logging camps is still there if you know where to look but it's fading. There used to be an old bucket, the bottom rusted out, lying on the ground on a flat area near a creek. I had rummaged around there and found a couple of horseshoes too. It must have been a stable area for the horses with water nearby. All that's gone now. Nature is reclaiming its own. There are three or four apple trees in an open area overlooking the Yellow Dog River. They're old and twisted and have obviously fought hard for survival. I often wonder who planted them there? and when? Maybe they grew from apple cores the lumberjacks dropped there. It's a likely spot. It might even be the camp from which those loggers and horses had to take refuge in the river.

I guess we're all just a very tiny part of a much bigger scheme of things. Enjoy life and move on. Better to pass through and leave no trace than to be the "S.O.B." who marked it with self-serving greed and garbage.

There have been stories about panning for gold in the Yellow Dog. I've tried it. All I ever succeeded in panning was iron ore.

Back at the cabin a small snake near the porch startles me. Seeing a snake is a kind of unsettling thing. I guess it's because you don't see it in the same way you become aware of other creatures. A person usually detects something because it moves. The snake is there and - suddenly - the thing that was there is gone - without apparent movement. I guess you have to have seen one to understand what I'm trying to say. It doesn't move like the rest of us. Stopping and looking closely I make out the snake, a grass snake, motionless and looking back at me. He's just a little thing, maybe a foot long. He, too, has his place to fill in the scheme of things. Go get 'em little fella. I won't bother you.

Rain! The shhhh of a gentle rain falling in the forest is a most peaceful sound. Not so hard that it rattles on the roof or thrashes the trees around with mighty gusting winds. It's just a soft steady watering of the woodland world with time for everything to drink long and slow and deep. Leaves flinch as a drop strikes them unexpectedly. Drops gather on the slender pine needles before dropping to the forest floor. Rivulets form on the roof, hesitate momentarily on the eaves of the cabin, then they plunge down to splash in a puddle below. Some few drops bounce musically on a forgotten sheet of tin just below the eaves. They're playing some unnamed symphony for the benefit of anyone who pauses to listen. If it has been a particularly warm day - or night - the soft cooling breeze that accompanies the rain is most welcome. When it rains it's a time for rest and reflection. So often we look upon rain as an obstacle, an harassment to our daily rush to fame, fortune, whatever. We should pause to receive it as replenishment and a time to relax. It's a time to consider where your life has been, where it's going, and why.

Evenings are most enjoyable, especially with a moon. Things can be heard but not seen and imagination often fills in the void. Bats can be glimpsed as they wheel and turn in pursuit of insects. They have a radar system that makes human effort appear infantile. A small fire is all that's required to keep away the "ghosties and ghoulies and long legged beasties and things that go 'bump' in the night."

Fire has always been fascination. It leaps and flickers cat-like on the wood it consumes – and – cat like, a person stares at it and wonders who is the master of whom. Fire has to be one of the oldest unchanged things in the world. Water lapping on a shore and fire dancing on a piece of wood have been in the world since long before we were. The first creature who peered fearfully from his hiding place at the first flame he had ever seen was looking at the same thing we are seeing today. It's as mysterious now as it was then. Discuss oxidation and combustibility but it remains a thing to be respected

The Northern Lights, Aurora Borealis, illuminate the night sky with curtains of light 600 miles high. When I was little they said it was the reflection of the midnight sun on the icebergs of the frozen north, blue and green and white. My father saw them red one night. The interpretation was that some ominous occurrence was coming. Now we're told the Northern Lights (and the Southern Lights - Aurora Australis) are caused by solar flares, nuclear eruptions on the sun. The eruptions create radioactive atomic particles that are blown on solar winds at speeds of 400 to 600 miles per second. Some particles are captured by the magnetic field of the Van Allen belt around the earth. They become visible where they are most concentrated - at the magnetic poles. I guess that explanation will have to do until the next theory comes along. Sit in the dark by your tiny campfire and look at that awesome display and feel pretty insignificant.

Later that evening I am wakened by a scuffling sound on the roof . What now? Should I get up - or not? I know that there are squirrels nesting in the leaves that insulate the ceiling but this doesn't sound like leaves. Kind of scratchy - and heavier than squirrels.

Dorothy is awake too. "What's that? There's something out there. What is it?" The long suffering lot of husbands the world over. Go find out what's making noises in the dark.

Flashlight in hand I climb a ladder to the shower tank on the porch roof, waving the beam wildly through the trees as I ascend. Peering over the eave the light catches two - no four - by golly there are eight little yellow reflectors shining back at me. A family of raccoons has climbed to the roof in an attempt to reach the bird feeders hanging in front of the window.

Dorothy climbs up behind me. "Aaaaw. They're raccoons! How cute."

The stars are brilliant. Polaris, the North Star, stands over the North Pole steady as a rock. The Big Dipper, on one side, points to it with the two pan-to-lip stars. The Chair of Cassiopeia, another star cluster spraddles on the other side. Memories return of sighting those stars through a sextant while crossing the Atlantic Ocean. It's kind of comforting to know the stars are still there. I wonder if someone is looking through a sextant at them right now? Ah well, back to bed.

Morning light creeps slowly through the windows into the cabin. The sun is below the horizon but some light diffuses through the atmosphere. Sunrise - sunset also - occurs much more slowly in the northern latitudes than it does near the equator. It's an angular thing. The sun shines more directly on the earth near the equator and a given amount of rotation results in a greater angular shift of the sun's rays. As one goes further north, for example, the setting and rising take longer until, at the pole in summer, the sun never sets at all. Anyway, in the early morning, I enjoy watching the sun come up. The woods come alive with the creatures of the day - birds, chipmunks, and hawks. Deer are often at the salt lick in the early light. I enjoy just watching them, seeing that they are here.

The coffee pot clucks and perks and fills the cabin with the aroma of fresh brewed coffee. I turn the fire down; pour a cup - darn - spilled a little. The pot hasn't drained down completely yet. Coffee in hand I sit on a bench outside and watch the sky change from very dark blue to a lighter and lighter shade. A few stray clouds on the eastern horizon take shape, catch the early rose-colored rays of the sun and blossom into gilt-edged gray. Trees, then branches and leaves slowly become visible. A few tentative chirps as a bird comes awake. A hungry chickadee lights on the feeder just a few feet away, looks me over, selects a sunflower seed and darts away to eat it.

Another day begins at the "Natural Elusion," our little cabin in the woods. I wonder what the rest of the world is doing?

♎

Brook Trout

This little brook trout jumped at one fly too many. No cause for concern. A minute or so after this picture was taken it had been released and was back in the pool.

Summer Rain

The wild raspberries are bursting out everywhere. Raspberry bushes are prolific. One or two planted in a suitable spot, almost anywhere with a little sun, and they'll spread. Blackberries are coming on strong. They're green and small at the moment but they'll turn red and, later, black. Blackberries are "red" when they're "green" you know. When they're black and ripe they're ever so sweet. The blackberry bushes are heavy with fruit.

Sugarplums and blueberries are ripening also. In the summer woods of Michigan's Upper Peninsula the livin' gets easy this time of year.

These days the bird feeders near our cabin don't need filling for extended periods of time. Everything seems to be "eating out." Earlier this spring those feeders would only last a day and a half before requiring a refill.

I was down by the beaver pond in front of our cabin the other day, tossing grasshoppers to the trout. Those 'hoppers don't last long once they've hit the water. One little trout, three or four inches long - looked like it might have been a brown trout - was so eager for that snack it shot clear out of the water. I'll bet it went six inches into the air after that prize. The competition in that pond is pretty stiff for juicy bugs. The difference between the "quick" and those who don't eat undoubtedly spurred his aerial acrobatics.

It's pleasant just sitting beside the pond, watching the fish rise for mosquitoes, grasshoppers, whatever. I've built a small slab desk and bench into the side of the pond bank; my "Office." It's an inspiring place to be.

An occasional cloud slides over the face of the sun – small, white, and puffy - and it's gone just as quickly. The bright sunlight sparkles on the rippling water like thousands of diamonds. The breeze lazily stirs the leaves overhead causing light and shadow to dance on the water. The sun's rays penetrate into the clear cold depths. There's a slight golden tinge to the water. The color is created by tannin, a chemical leached from bark and the plants the water has filtered through. Even the bugs are cooperating and aren't bothering me much. It's a lazy, pleasant, peaceful day.

Then the light seems to fade - just a little. Not a sudden thing but a slow, gradual darkening. Maybe, had I been watching more closely, I would have noticed the change sooner. The wind has stopped completely. Everything is quiet, still.

Looking up I see a dark, foreboding cloud approaching from the west. It's dirty gray looking and puffy.

Sunshine and shadows are no longer dancing on the surface of the pond. The sparkling diamonds are gone. It's quiet. Nothing moves. A lone bird chirps briefly in the distance and suddenly stops. The leaves are motionless, even the popples, the quaking aspens, with their delicately balanced leaf and stem system - are motionless. I strain to hear any sound. Nothing! No movement!

I gather my things and start back to the cabin. At the cabin I close the windows in my truck, gather tools that had been scattered about and put them inside the shed. Then it's time for me to take cover inside the cabin.

A large pot of soup simmers on the back burner of the stove. Dorothy often makes a large pot of soup and keeps it on the stove. It doesn't require refrigeration if, once each day, it's heated, allowed to simmer for ten minutes or so, then let cool again. Maintained that way, it'll theoretically keep forever. Actually, that's a lie. As good as that soup is, it doesn't last long at all. Strange – or maybe not so strange? It seems to taste better and better with each passing day. At the moment, the aroma of that simmering soup fits right in with the approaching dark cloud. It's like a security blanket.

I wash up at the sink; ladle out a bowl of that hot soup, and go sit out on the front porch. The porch has a roof with the sides open except for screens. Our shower bath is on the porch. I lug a bucket of hot water onto the roof and pour it into a tank on the roof. A pipe runs through the roof to a valve and shower head below. Dorothy had me screen the porch against mosquitoes.

The soup is hot. Sitting back in a big armchair I blow gently on the soup and listen to the quiet. It's times like this a person's just gotta believe in God.

Our nearest neighbor, human neighbor, is "Yellow Dog Bill!" He has a camp about a mile and a quarter away, through the woods. He stays up here, he and his dog, for the same reasons we do I guess: he likes the solitude.

There's another "sometime" neighbor about a half mile away down the trail. I think the guy would like to stay up here, summers at least, but his wife is involved with the flower club and the lady's tea society and the other local civic make-everything-nice committees. They do have a nice home in Marquette but there's nothing in town that's as nice as it is up here.

Tap! Tap-tap! Tap-tap-tap-tappety tap tap!

I pause, spoon in midair, and listen. The sounds are gentle but persistent. They quickly pick up in tempo. Rain! A maple leaf on a nearby tree bounces in surprise as a raindrop hits it. A blade of grass suddenly flicks downward and, just as quickly, bounces back up again.

A drop of water - then two - seven or eight fall from the eaves. Soon there's the steady rat-tat-tat of water droplets striking the bottom of the empty rain barrel. In the background the original tap-tap-tap of individual raindrops has blended into a soft steady roar on the forest canopy. The sod I just laid against the bank by the creek will welcome this shower.

A drop of water strikes my right shoulder. Peering upward I see a wet spot on the underside of the porch roof. I make a mental note to get up there with the bucket of roof sealer as soon as things dry out again.

A steady stream of water now runs from the gutter along the eave. It splashes and chortles into what has become a reservoir of water in the rain barrel.

Slowly I sip my soup and listen to the splendor of this rain-conducted opera sounding forth all around me.

The rain slackens slightly. The music diminishes. It gets noticeably brighter. The rattling tympani in the rain barrel slows. Individual drops now echo and reverberate in the hollow acoustic of the large drum. A blue jay's harsh shriek pierces the damp stillness.

The rain has stopped. It was a brief shower but there's a fresh clean smell in the woods. Colors are more distinct. Shadows stand out more clearly. The rain has washed the dust from the air and deepened the accent between contrasting colors. A crow flies overhead cawing, plaintive, wet, and alone. My soup bowl is empty. My belly is full. Contentment surrounds me. How did I get so lucky? I've got a quietly beautiful place and a snug cabin in the woods. I have a wife who seems to like this rustic life as much as I do.

As I ruminate, a chipmunk climbs up on the back of one of the slab chairs outside. It's a little wet, licking its fur, grooming itself after the rain. Ah, well, some neighbors are nice to have.

Here comes the sunshine again. Rain drops clinging to pine needles sparkle like diamonds. A water droplet, gathered in the hollow of a dogbane leaf, retains its spherical shape. There must be natural wax or oils on the leaf I guess. When the sun hits it the droplet refracts the light, glowing like a pearl. Clear, clean, fresh water! That's a real pearl - a "pearl of great price." There's gotta be a God out there somewhere - and I think he's talking to me.

℧

Memories on a Summer Night

The tenth of August was a full moon. Too often the weather doesn't cooperate with the lunar cycle but August 10 was outstanding. It was about two o'clock in the morning and outside it was light enough to read a newspaper. I went for a walk. I must have strolled around for an hour or more. It was beautiful! Nobody was there but me. There may have been animals going about their normal lives but they seemed to have no interest in my wandering. They didn't bother me and, if I bothered them, they didn't say anything.

The moonlight seems - I don't know - "softer" when a person is alone in beautiful surroundings. The shadows are deeper. It's wonderfully quiet. The trunk of an old scarred pine tree stands out, highlighted by moonlight, tall and straight against a shadowy background. The crown of the tree is silhouetted, darker than the indigo sky behind it. It looks regal. The scars on the trunk and any dead branches are hidden. Everything is beautiful by moonlight. There's more latitude for imagination - less detail of reality.

Memories of other moonlight nights drift through my mind. Soaring high in the sky in a B-47 jet bomber on the way to England. Over the ocean there was no sense of movement even though we were traveling at several hundred miles per hour.

Those stars up there, sighted through a sextant, were our signposts then. Another moonlit night in the cockpit of an F-4 Phantom jet fighter over Southeast Asia snuggled up close to a tanker aircraft for fuel. The tanker's huge shadow was darker than the surrounding sky while the red and green navigation lights blink on and off making one think of Christmas. It was beautiful. Unfortunately we were on our way to go "down someone's chimney" and blow someone up. It makes a terrible conflict between surroundings and purpose.

A happier time was when my son, Benny, and I walking the winter woods from the Yellow Dog River followed the North Star to our cabin. The moon was bright that night too.

Other nights drift across my memory. Other nights - other places - just me and the moon.

A neighbor's dog took a halfhearted interest in my passing. Not for long. Even the dog seemed intimidated by the beauty of the night.

Flowers beside the road are visible, even the colors. Maybe it's because I know where they are. Even though I can see the flowers and the grass and the bushes, the rest, the discarded cigarette lighter, the empty drink cups, the beer cans, all seem hidden. They're still there, if you look hard, but they're not apparent. The whole world seems prettier by moonlight.

Another memory. Many years ago - many MANY years ago - a young lady and I were gazing at the moon from a parked car in an Illinois cornfield. It was a beautiful night for - er - lunar observation. After a period of silence staring at the velvet sky, the moon, and the stars, she asked, "Can you see the outline of a man and a woman about to embrace, about to kiss, in the face of the moon?" She went on to explain that only those who are truly in love are able see it. I saw it. I really did see it that night. Next time the moon is full see if you can see it. Look for that picture - not so much a "picture" as an impression. See if you can see it. The moon rotates at a rate that matches its speed around the earth so the same side of the moon always faces earth. That couple is always there in the moon ready to embrace. If any of you guys check it out with your spouse, and if you don't see it, I suggest you lie.

Moonlight on the water! That's got to bring back memories to everyone. One night in Alabama Dorothy and I were anchored out in a small sailboat on a Gulf of Mexico inlet. We'd been asleep but I woke up at - I don't know what time it was - late. There was a soft breeze - just enough to ripple the water. It created a sparkling jeweled pathway under the full moon. I woke Dorothy. She made some hot chocolate and we just sat there looking at the beauty around us. There was no reason to speak. Hollywood used to make movies with scenes like that. In today's movies I guess they'd have to shoot someone and blow the boat up.

The moon is beautiful wherever you see it but artificial light - street lights – cities - all seem to dilute it. A peek out the window doesn't do it either. You've got to be ". . .out in the great alone when the moon is bright and clear. . .with a silence you most could hear. . ." by yourself - or with someone who can see that couple embracing in the moon too.

♎

Aurora Borealis

The Aurora Borealis, the Northern Lights; The illumination of radioactive particles in a solar wind captured by the earth's magnetic field.

Lights in the Northern Sky

We had visitors from Texas a few days ago. My daughter, LeAnne, son-in-law Glenn Bearden, and granddaughter Christi Lee Robinson made a whirlwind trip through Upper Michigan. They managed two days with us in Marquette. The beautiful sights and sounds of our Upper Peninsula are quite foreign to their environment in Fort Worth.

On their first night here I awoke about five o'clock in the morning (who knows why those things happen?) and glanced out our north-facing bedroom window. There, in the clear and starry northern sky, curling and twisting and turning, were those curtains of yellowish-green light familiar to north country dwellers. We know them as the "Northern Lights" - Aurora Borealis! We're fortunate at our house to have a sweeping view across Lake Superior revealing a broad swath of the northern sky.

I hadn't seen the Northern Lights - golly - for years. They were there, I'm sure, but I was asleep. I jumped out of bed, bumped into; I don't know what but it woke Dorothy. I told her to look out the window as I pulled on slippers and robe and hurried to wake our guests.

They got up immediately and everybody gathered on the porch oohing and aahing and pointing. LeAnne asked, "Daddy, how does that happen?"

"Well, honey, I knew you all would be here so I called up and arranged . . ." There was a time, when she was little, that she might have believed that. She had just celebrated her thirtieth birthday A few weeks earlier and had long since lost that "daddy knows everything" aura. I didn't need any more light than already existed to know she wasn't swallowing my story. I wonder if Christie Lee might? As we watched and talked they realized that seeing this display this far south of the Polar Regions was a privileged experience.

When I was a youngster I remember folks speculating that those curtains of color were sunlight reflecting off the icebergs of the far north. These days the scientific types tell us it's the result of radioactive particles blown by a solar wind from hydrogen eruptions on the sun. The charged particles are captured by the earth's magnetic fields and concentrated at the poles. The radioactive excitation of earth's oxygen atoms creates that familiar yellow-green glow. Nitrogen atoms, they say, create a red glow. The activity usually occurs from the magnetic pole to approximately 20 degrees latitude, north or south. The band of light is only a couple miles thick (north to south) but can stretch east to west for thousands of miles. The lower edge may be 50 miles up but can extend upwards to a couple hundred miles.

There's an 11-year solar eruption cycle that is believed to create periods of greater electro-magnetic radiation. Then there's an ebbing and flooding of the intensity that seems to correspond to the 27 day time-of-rotation of the sun. Another factor seems to be periods of solstice - the sun at its most northern (or southern) latitude: June (or December). It's then that the poles (north or south) are more closely aligned toward the sun itself.

Don't you feel a lot smarter now, knowing all that? Now let me tell you the real story.

"Aurora" is the goddess of the dawn. She drives six white horses and a chariot over the eastern horizon each morning, dispersing the darkness with her rosy fingers. She sheds the first soft light of day on the earth. Aurora is the mother of the winds and the sister of Helios, the sun, who rides across the heavens lighting the day. In that time before dawn Aurora sometimes leads Helios in a circle of the poles. Their light reflects off the polar ice upward into the atmosphere.

"Aurora Borealis" means Lights of the North. South of the equator it's called " Aurora Australis."

Occasionally those reflections can extend down to 60 degrees of latitude – they can cover the whole sky. I've seen it and it's spectacular! You'll have to get up in the dark though. The wee hours of the morning are best.

You can believe my story - or you can listen to rumor mongers like Copernicus and Galileo. Ask yourself, would I lie to you?

♎

The People

They call us "Yoopers." The name comes from the letters "U.P." indicating the "Upper Peninsula," of Michigan. To most people from lower Michigan, northern Michigan ends at the Mackinac Bridge, short of God's country.

People from south of the bridge, we Yoopers call them "Trolls" (people who live "down below" the bridge), look upon us Yoopers as a sort of an illegitimate child. There have even been movements now and then for us (the U.P.) to secede (from Michigan, not the USA).

Areas of the world have characteristics that make them different, unique. Even so there are areas of our country that have characteristics that make them unique. We, in the Upper Peninsula, may just have a few characteristics of our own – besides the expression, "Yah, sure, you betcha!" Ours is a hard land that produces strong offspring. When the going gets tough, as it occasionally does, especially during winter months, our people pull together for the mutual good. Oh we've got a few SOBs, just to flavor the stew, but we've got some pretty good folk also. Read on and see what you think.

Ω

Come On Along

Why I Live in Michigan's Upper Peninsula

If you happened to be in Michigan's Upper Peninsula and were talking to a native of the area you might ask them why they live in the U.P. Their first reaction might be a puzzled stare. Then, maybe their eyes would narrow and their face would take on a thoughtful expression. Their shoulders might shrug with uncertainty and they'd heave a sigh. Then their head would cock to one side, and their reply would probably start, "Well, I'll tell you . . ."

"Code blue! Code blue!" "Emergency! Emergency!"

Here's the situation: You're standing at the swinging doorway of an operating room at one of our local hospitals. The doctor has "scrubbed in" and stands with gloved hands held in the air (just like on the TV). The operating room staff, the nurses, the anesth . . . anethis . . . the anisti . . . you know, the one who gives you the gas (or whatever) that takes you "out-of-it" –, they all stand ready in masks and caps and hospital "greens." Overhead the intense lights of the operating room illuminate everything in bright, white light. Sterilized instruments lie on a cloth-covered tray in readiness for the upcoming procedure. A surgical nurse waits to pass them to the surgeon's hand as he requests them. Flexible tubing and pumps and tiny electric wires lead to monitoring equipment. There's a faint

195

hum in the background. All is in readiness. The antisept . . . antithist . . . ann - ess - thit . . . - you know - is poised to do his thing. With everyone in this heightened state of readiness, what is it that's holding things up?"

The patient, the subject of all this preparation lies under a sheet on a gurney. Two attendants are in the process of pushing the gurney through the open door when, "No! Stop! Wait!"

The doctor turns around with a puzzled expression on his face. The attendants halt in the doorway, confused. The staff cast uncertain glances at one another. The doctor approaches the gurney, looks down at the patient then glances inquiringly at the antist . . . anti - you know who I mean. Shoulders shrug in bewilderment, shaking his head in the negative.

Bending down over the patient, and in a most soothing bedside manner, the doctor asks, "What is it?"

"My dog!"

Again everyone exchanges bewildered glances, puzzled looks, shrugging at one another.

"What about the dog," asks the doctor?

"I'll be gone. What if I don't . . .?" Eyes look beseechingly at the masked face of this healer of all things.

The doctor attempts to sooth this patients concern. "Don't worry. You're going to be fine."
"But my dog? Someone has to take care of my dog?"

The patient is an elderly gentleman with no immediate family. During a routine scheduled visit it was abruptly discovered that he needed surgery – now!

Preliminary events overtook the old gentleman - whirling by - confusing - out of his control. The medical system moved smoothly, efficiently, inexorably carrying him toward the sharp blade of the surgeon's knife! He's alone. Events are moving beyond him and he's feeling helpless – and afraid. He's the central focus of all these quiet, efficient, germ-free and masked strangers - and he's scared. His thoughts turn to his faithful companion, a dependent, his nearest and dearest friend. "If I'm not there, who'll take care of my dog?"

A dog? All this modern high-tech efficiency has been brought to a stand still by – a dog?

The pregnant silence was broken when the doctor called for a cellular telephone.

"Who shall I call?"

"Call my neighbor, 'XXXX'."

The telephone number of "XXXX" is found in a directory. The number is dialed, and the phone rings - and rings - and rings again. It looked like . .

"Hello?"

"Hello. Is this 'XXXX'?"

"Yes, it is."

"This is Doctor "so-and-so." Mr. "so-and-so" (no relation) is here, in the hospital, about to undergo surgery. He's concerned about - well - I'll let you talk to him."

The phone is held to the patients ear. "Hello? My dog is in the house - alone - and I can't - - -" Information is passed; the hiding place of the door key, the character of the dog, the location of the dog food and the amount required - and when. What time the dog likes to go for a walk - scratch behind the ears - etc. etc. - all the particulars.

When all the details have been passed, acknowledged, and agreed to, the anesti - (you know) - took the phone: "If there's still a problem, you can call a social worker who'll . . ."

The patient, now more relaxed, was wheeled into the operating room. The surgery was performed quietly and efficiently and all went well. At home the dog had been fed, taken for a walk, his ears were scratched, (some "doo-doo" cleaned up) and he is as perky and active as ever.

Now don't hold me too close to the details of this story but it's fundamentally correct. Everyone involved had gone that extra little bit. We may never know how much of a difference that might have made. As it turned out, "XXXX" was a former patient and known by the doctor. The social worker was Mr. "so and so's" dentist's wife. This all came out subsequent to the incident itself. The dog was - well - he was a dog. He was "man's best friend" and found that he too, had friends, friends that he had never met.

Yes, this Upper Peninsula of Michigan is a beautiful land. There are the very distinctive seasons (especially the fall colors) - and the forests and the lakes and the rivers and - and - and there's the people. As there are everywhere, there are good people and bad people and probably a few that are indifferent. But there are some among us who are really good. And who knows, maybe some of that'll rub off on the rest of us? This is our Upper Peninsula and . . and . . . What was your original question again?

♎

Come On Along

"Good Lookin' Tom"

There are things that catch a person's eye when just
wandering. Look further. There's history and human
determination under that stone.

"Good Lookin' Tom"

It's funny what you see sometimes when you
least expect it, something that attracts your
attention. I chanced to be in a cemetery one day
away up in Big Bay in Michigan's Upper Peninsula.
An inscription on a particular headstone caught my
eye: "Good Looking Tom." It was a quiet day,
summer, I don't know what I was doing in the
cemetery - just wandering and wondering. There's a
lot of history – and the dates of the history - in a
cemetery. Of course the folks you meet aren't very
talkative but there's a lot to be learned there anyway

if you'll just look. "Good Looking Tom," for example. Who are you, Tom? And what's the "Good Looking" all about? Tom didn't say. I guess I'll have to ask around.

The full name on the marker was Thomas Procyk. The dates were 1897 - 1985. The story as I discovered it began about 1911 in Russia – somewhere in Siberia. Tom's father was Russian. His mother was from Kiev, in Poland. Tom was 14 years old and life was a bummer. I don't mean "bummer" as in, "My momma makes me study, I can't watch TV." It was, "There's nothing to study, darn little to eat, and the long hard hours of labor every day grind a person right into the frozen ground." America, Tom had heard, was the place to go. Get there any way you can. This was his mother talking to him. She told him he should go. Tom and another young fella', John Cozak, left home and family at the tender age of 14. They never looked back.

The boys worked their way to a port on the Bering Sea and were able, by hook or by crook, to get aboard a boat heading for Alaska. Alaska had been known as "Russian America" 'til William Seward, Secretary of State under President Abraham Lincoln, bought it for the United States in 1867 in a transaction popularly called "Seward's Folly." In 1911 traffic back and forth between the two countries was still a common thing. The distance was only 60 miles across the Bering Straits.

When they arrived in Alaska the two boys

jumped ship, searched for, and took whatever jobs would put something in their bellies. Life was still pretty hard. These two young graduates of survival in Siberian Russia were already familiar with "hard." The days ran to months, to years with them working on fishing boats, in salmon canneries, wherever and at whatever they could do. Gradually they drifted southward through Canada. They worked on the railroad for a while. Tom even worked in a salt mine.

Then the Great War started in Europe. Tom was fearful Russia would want him back. He had no passport or Canadian citizenship. He had no wish to return to Russia. He heard that if he would join the United States Army he could, in exchange for "good and faithful service," receive citizenship in the United States. Maybe this was the start of the army's "Be All That You Can Be?"

After serving with the Army Tom received his discharge, his citizenship and found himself at loose ends in Detroit. There he met another kind of recruiter, a fella the trades called "a man catcher."

Man catchers were sent by business interests needing manpower to population centers to recruit workers. The Big Bay logging company had such a need. Tom was recruited and came to Big Bay. He worked in a logging camp for a while, then at the sawmill there and in between at whatever work he could find. One of the jobs Tom found was as a handyman around the construction site of Mr. And Mrs. Louis G. Kaufman's Granot Loma lodge.

Mr. Louis G. Kaufman was a successful banker with interests that were nationwide. Granot Loma was to be their palatial lodge on Lake Superior. Tom worked at whatever was assigned to him, landscaping, labor, whatever was called for. Mrs. Kaufman put Tom to work one day aligning stones, boulders, along each side of the entrance road running from the village of Birch (near what is now Halfway location) several miles to the main lodge.

Louis Kaufman drove by one day and stopped. "What in @#% are you doing?"
"Puttin' these stones along the road," Tom replied.
"Well don't do that. Get 'em out of there!"

Tom began removing the stones. An hour or so later Mrs. Kaufman came by and saw what Tom was doing. She too stopped long enough to shout from the car, "Put those stones along the road like I asked." Pointing at the road's edge she said "Put them along there."

A couple hours later she passed by again. Nothing had been done. Tom was gone. Mrs. Kaufman went looking for Tom. She finally found him sitting in Maude's beer hall in Big Bay.

"Why aren't you working," she asked?

Tom shook his head in disgust. "You say put the rocks down. The Mister say pick the rocks up. You come and say put the rocks back." He shook his head again, "There's too many bosses."

"Well you just listen to me! I'm the boss at Granot Loma. If Louis tells you different you tell him to talk to me!" Tom went back to lining the road with stones.

Tom continued to live in and around Big Bay, working at whatever he could. As he got older the Temples, Earl and Vernice, looked after him, helped him get to his doctor appointments, saw that he had something to eat. That's the way it is up here in the woods. Folks look after one another.

Tom received much of his medical attention from a Veteran's Facility in Marquette because of his service during World War I. He received a heart pacemaker in one operation. When the unit wore out and malfunctioned he returned to the facility to get a replacement.

With his new pacemaker working properly, Tom looked for one of the nurses that had been particularly kind and considerate. When he found her, he placed his old pacemaker in her hand and said, "Here. I give you my heart."

Tom died in 1985. He never did return to Russia. He never saw nor heard from either of his parents since his mother sent him away at age 14: "Go to America – any way you can get there."

Mrs. Kaufman gave the "Good Looking" prefix to Tom's name. I guess it was Mrs. Kaufman's way of differentiating him from another worker named Tom. Tom was so proud of that name he asked that it be put on his tombstone.

I can't help but wonder - was there an "Ugly Tom?"

Ω

Come On Along

Lonesome Whistle

The railroad tracks out behind my home are rusty. They're still covered with snow in some spots. They stretch out into the distance as far as the eye can see. They seem to come together – somewhere away out there. There hasn't been a train by here since, gosh, I don't remember when. It's been a long time.

Those rails used to be the steel bands that bound the nation together. They used to be. Once upon a time the strident cry of a steam whistle announced the coming of civilization to a wild and unsettled country.

It was the sound of progress reaching out across the broad grassland of the midwest and the forests of northern Michigan.

It echoed from the restrictive canyon walls of the Rocky Mountains. It rolled melodiously across the expanse of the Pacific Ocean, fading into that vast distance. That was once upon a time.

I can remember the resting "whishhh" of escaping steam as the train stood in the station, the jangle of its bell. The engine was motionless, quietly awaiting the conductor's signal, his swinging lantern to signal the engineer. His cry to the passengers of "All Abooooard!"

The engineer would gently move the throttle, the "Johnson Bar," forward releasing live steam into mighty sealed cylinders. The huge connecting rod stirs as the piston responds to the pressure. A sweating fireman heaves coal into the roaring firebox. The controlled might of that high-pressure steam leans into the task of moving the huge engine and its attached cars.

Massive counterweighted drive wheels begin to rotate. Steam vents suddenly in a mighty exhalation as the driving piston reaches the limit of its travel. Valves direct the steam to reverse the piston's direction. The connecting rod moves back again. The wheels turn. "Choo!" A short pause. "Choo!' Again and again and again it goes. The couplings between the cars bang individually as forward motion takes up the slack in each one. Each car, in its turn, lurches forward. Standing passengers caught unaware, grab anything handy for support. The drive wheels accelerate their rotation.

It takes a gentle but firm hand on the Johnson Bar. Too much power too fast can cause the straining drive wheels to slip. When this happens, those huge, weighted wheels spin - "choo-choo-choo" - until the engineer eases the bar back. When the wheels regain traction the "choo" resumes its slow acceleration as the train picks up speed. As it moves faster and faster the "breathing" of the engine becomes a rapid, steady staccato of unchained energy.

Pistons, rods, and valves function at speeds that baffle the imagination. To climax this maddening cacophony of rolling wheels, flailing valves, and surging pistons comes the unique, haunting wail of the steam whistle. The engineer, leaning forward in the cab, pulls the cord that activates a valve releasing steam pressure to blow the whistle. The wailing sound warns all, far and near, that the train is coming - watch out!

Each engineer developed and was proud of his own "feel" for the whistle. Each whistle, due to its construction, leverage, friction, the wear of the linkage, the pressure in the boiler, had its own unique voice. Add to that the touch of an engineer's hand and the ensuing sound can be distinctively unique to a discerning ear. That individual whistle sound - the variation, the tone, the "feel" of the hand on the cord - and many of the "old timers" might remark, "That's Casey with ole number nine. He's bottoming out the grade about now." Then they'd pull at the fob hanging from a vest pocket and peer down at a huge old railroader's watch. Nodding his head he'd say, "I believe he'll bring 'er in on time."

In the thirties, during the despair of the dust bowl and the grinding poverty of the great depression, trains were one of the few constants that remained. Men roamed the land searching for work that didn't exist. Families struggled to survive. There was no unemployment compensation in those days, no social security. There were some "relief" programs, maybe a soup kitchen, and some charities. The men – and some of the women - searched for anything to earn a little money to send home. Those rails made pretty straight lines from one town to another and the people followed them.

"Tie counters," they were called, walking the rails, "counting" the railroad ties. If a passing train wasn't moving too fast - still in the train yard or maybe climbing a grade - folks might take a chance and try to swing aboard. The railroad employed security guards, "Railroad Dicks" (detectives), to protect the cargoes. Some of these enforcers were strict. Some were not so strict. Some carried clubs and were mean.

These were hard times. Men were expected to be the providers, the head of the family - and they couldn't - and they weren't - and they wondered where they had "failed" - and no one could tell them. Philosophical conjecture was the idle pastime of the fortunate few - the "academicians." For the mass of people the very real threat of starvation overshadowed these theoretical trivialities. Families were torn apart emotionally and physically. Life was typified by those hard steel rails that stretched out to – where? Away off in the distance it all seemed to come together - away out there - somewhere.

A whole generation grew up associating that mournful train whistle in the night with lonesome - desperation - fear. Men, women, and children wandered hungry along those miles of cold, unfeeling steel. Women struggled to provide hope for their children while anxiously watching for those trains, hoping for some word from their men. These men and women often went without themselves to provide a meager ration for their children.

An unassuming monument to those times, a symbol, still exists in Marquette, in Michigan's Upper Peninsula. The rail yard on south Front Street is vacant, abandoned now. The huge rock on the lakeshore beside the yard, "Gaines Rock," was where these searchers, these "tie counters," these hoboes, would gather to sustain and support one another. They'd go gathering, searching, foraging, and begging around town. When they returned they'd combine their meager findings in a common cauldron over an open fire. They'd make soup. Beside them was the rail yard, the trains, the endless tracks that always promised to come together out there - somewhere. And away off in the distance a whistle would moan its homesick wail into the uncaring darkness of a lonely night.

Those were times no one would wish for anyone. They were the white-hot forges in which many melted but from which some emerged stronger for the experience. Those hardships were swept away by the industrial demand of the great World War II. Hard times have diminished, were never known by later generations, but they haven't disappeared. For many who lived through them, they never will.

Those rails that stretched their promise off into the distance are now thought to be obsolete. In many areas they've been torn up. Those rails, those steel bands that held a people together.

My generation, the one that listened to that lonely whistle, is passing. There aren't many of us left. If we start a tale with, "Back when I was a kid . . ." we're tuned out - turned off - shut down. The new generation has a home, two cars, a stereo with volume that will shatter glass, and a taste for self-indulgence that can't be satisfied. I wonder if they, too, may one day discover that those tracks never do come together out there.

♎

Art Keeler

It happened not long after I graduated from high school. I was 19 years old and the draft for the Korean War was on my trail. Although I didn't know it yet, in a few short months I would be in the United States Air Force.

Art Keeler had been around a long time and was fast approaching senior citizen status. He had been a mechanic for more years than I had been alive. He'd probably forgotten more about automobiles, tractors, generators, and all things mechanical than I knew or, as it turned out, ever would know. When I entered the Air Force they sent me to a radio repair school, then to pilot training, and I never did get back to things mechanical. But this is not supposed to be about me. It's about Art Keeler and a chapter in my education.

Art was a rough old cob. If you crossed him you were in big trouble. If you were sincerely trying to pull your own weight, doing your best, he was a good friend. He and I got along fine. We wound up working together (me working for him, that is) "on the road," as they say. We worked for a heavy equipment sales and service outfit. Somebody else did the selling and the delivery. Art and I got called when things weren't going well. We took care of servicing what was sold. We would be working together for several months – 'til the military draft pushed me into the Air Force. This is the story of a lesson in life taught during one of our service calls.

A sawmill in the woods north of Marquette and west of Big Bay in Michigan's Upper Peninsula had bought a large six-cylinder diesel power plant. It powered the entire mill, saw, planer, bull chain, everything. The engine had been installed and was up and running. After a few days the user discovered it was leaking prodigious quantities of lubricating oil. A 'phone call to the company with a cry for help generated a work order. That sent Art and I on our way to the woods.

This was November, late fall in upper Michigan. The temperature was in the low teens. Snow was coming down in small hard pellets that the wind was blowing almost horizontally. When we arrived at the sawmill we found the unit was mounted on a heavy timber frame under a tin roof - but without any walls. An inch or so of lubricating oil had gathered under the unit covering the oil soaked earth. The leak was soon traced to a seal around the forward main crankshaft bearing. Guess who got the job of lying on the ground underneath that unit to remove the engine oil pan. There was no way to "tip-toe" around the situation. It was down and dirty and wet and cold and miserable. . The fault turned out to be a poorly installed oil seal, a mistake at the factory. Art, with typical foresight, had brought a seal with us. The faulty seal was quickly and easily removed and the new seal was installed – correctly. Now, who would lie back down in that frigid mess to replace that oil pan? You already know the answer, don't you? Fortunately it slipped back into place quite easily. Although my fingers had lost their sense of feel, the bolts were large and I had minimal trouble replacing them all and re-installing the oil pan.

We must have been there for two or three hours. When we got ready to leave the back of my coveralls, my (long) underwear, and my hide, I believe, were thoroughly soaked with oil. Cold, wet, dirty engine oil. The little heater in the cab of our pickup truck just wasn't doing the job. An old jacket and a handful of rags kept me from leaking oil all over the seat of the truck but did very little to help me get warm. I was miserable.

Art happened to have another work order he'd picked up just before we left the garage. It was for a place up in the same area as the sawmill. He thought we'd take care of it on our way home. It was to repair a generator at a little backwoods bar called "The Halfway Tavern." It wasn't really halfway to anywhere but it was between Marquette and Big Bay and that was close enough to give it the name. It catered to thirsty lumberjacks, end-of-the-day truck drivers, tired loggers and the occasional wayward repair crew - us.

Commercial electricity had not yet reached Halfway. It would be several years before it finally arrived. Louis Malnor, the bar owner, had long depended on a generator he had purchased from us.

It provided the only source of light and power for his home and for the tavern and it had stopped working. Quite understandably he wanted it repaired "as soon as possible."

It was dark before Art and I finally pulled up in front of the Halfway Tavern. I was cold, really cold, darn near in a stupor. I would have had to feel better to die. My back was raw from the oil-wet clothing and the jiggling of the truck over the back roads. We walked into the bar – well, Art walked. I kind of shuffled.

There were two lumberjacks drinking beer in a back booth by the light of a kerosene lantern. Two more lanterns lit the bar area. Louis stood, arms folded behind the bar.

Art strode up to the bar in his usual extroverted manner, slapped his hand on the counter and demanded, "Give us a drink!"

Louis slowly moved down the bar, wiping the counter as he came, and looking closely at me. He turned toward Art, jerked his head in my direction and asked, "How old is that kid?"

Now Michigan requires a person have attained the age of twenty-one years before buying or consuming any alcoholic beverage. I didn't say anything. I just stood there, miserable, and deep-freeze cold.

Art didn't flinch or waver. He leaned across the bar, looked Louis right in the eye, and asked, "Do you want your generator fixed?"

Louis kind of paused, looking at Art in

surprise. I guess he decided Art wasn't kidding. He glanced around – there was no one else there but the two lumberjacks. He turned and reached for a bottle.

A couple hours later the generator was humming contentedly, the lights were burning brightly, Louis wore a broad smile, and I wasn't cold anymore. I didn't know if I was afoot or horseback but I wasn't cold.

Art got me home that night. I think he did? I guess if a person is going to grow up in the woods, work around logging camps and sawmills, and frequent those lumberjack bars, things like that are an occupational hazard. It was part of growing up in upper Michigan.

♎

Come On Along

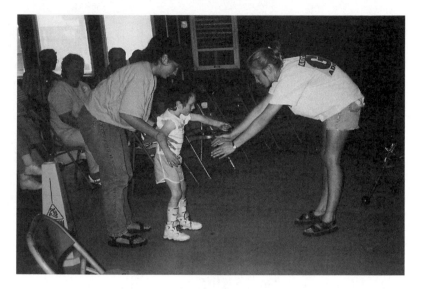

Courage!
Amanda Hakola strives to be all that she can be.
Bay Cliff Health Camp's counselors offer
encouragement. Bay Cliff, a place "Where
dreams come true!" They really do.

Courage and High Achievement

A birthday party was held one evening in Big Bay, Michigan, about 30 miles north of Marquette. The reports of successes at the Olympic games held that year in Atlanta, Georgia, were in the news that morning. You may be wondering what the connection could be. Let me tell you how these seemingly unrelated events have a common thread.

At the Olympic games a young lady was competing in the breast stroke swimming event.

219

She was told not to. She was told she didn't have a chance. She entered anyway.

Another young lady, a gymnast, competed with an ankle injury. She finished the event in great pain, standing on one leg. She had to drag herself off the mat on her hands and knees.

Guess who the winners of these events were? In the north country that's called Guts! Will! Courage! What folks of Finnish ancestry refer to as "Sisu!" You just can't stop them.

Now to the Birthday Party. This would be the 63rd anniversary of the founding of Bay Cliff Health Camp. I'll pause here to tell you a little about Bay Cliff, the reason it exists, so you can make the connection.

Sixty-three years ago Miss Elba Morse, a Registered Nurse, and Doctor Goldie Corneliuson, a Medical Doctor, transformed a former dairy farm into a children's care facility. Their original goal was to provide a summer camp for underprivileged and undernourished children. It's important to recognize that these two courageous women initiated this plan back in the 1930s. Not only was it more difficult to raise money for this project – donations, grants, whatever – at this time but there were innumerably more "underprivileged and undernourished" children. The country was in the grip of the great depression. There was no work to be had, no unemployment compensation or welfare programs, and a multitude of people, old and young, with little or nothing to eat. Their concern was the future – and the future was the children. It was a bold undertaking and these two women made it work.

The Bay Cliff program has since expanded to include children who are impaired, disabled, crippled – whatever you choose as the politically correct term. The main focus of Bay Cliff was and continues to be the children. I could go on about those two courageous and far-sighted ladies and even more about the dedicated folks who have followed them. It would be about dedication, heart, caring, and love - a lot about love. It would also be about Guts! Will! Courage! "Sisu!" For that part we're going to talk about the kids.

They come in all shapes and sizes and impediments, those kids - and all colors too. Some are repeaters - they've been here before. For others it's their first time. When they arrive the first order of business is to send all parents, relatives, etc. home! "Don't come back 'til it's over." Some parents, loved ones, often find that hard to accept. To them I would say, "Wrong!" If I could arrange it I'd have a couple of those guys from Chicago - you know - the ones in fedoras and overcoats with noses pushed to one side - call on you and make you "an offer you couldn't refuse."

Bay Cliff has a staff and counselors carefully selected from numerous applicants – and there are many applicants. They watch over the kids. The ratio of counselor to camper may be 5:1, or it may be 1:1 – determined solely by the need of the child.

I didn't say they "take care of" the kids, although they do.

"Take care of" would give the wrong connotation. At the risk of alienating parents and caregivers everywhere I would say these Bay Cliff children have never received better care in their lives. This is not the cloying "take care of" or "don't let anything happen to" or "poor little - " whoever. This care is designed to – well - the Army-recruiting slogan says it best: "Be All That You Can Be!"

Well-meaning parents want to shield the child against failure. They don't ask him (or her) to try to talk - or walk - or whatever the impairment. They fear they may fail. So what? The tragedy is not failing, the tragedy is in never trying. Look at the many accomplishments of people who weren't afraid to fail. Look beyond. Look to Bay Cliff. It's "The place where dreams come true."

At Bay Cliff everything is geared to "can," to succeeding, to what's possible. Whatever they're doing - reading stories, making craft projects, singing songs, whatever - the emphasis is positive. The question is not, "Why?" The question is, "Why not?"

And the kids are infected with this "can do" virus. They lose sight of the idea that they "can't." A little girl with braces on both her legs but with the biggest smile on her face is just burning out the bearings on her walker. A young fella in an electric wheelchair is lighting up the whole area with his enthusiasm. One youngster came to Bay Cliff in a wheelchair and now, well, the wheel chair is gathering dust in the basement. He changed from a shy, withdrawn child to an extrovert that would put a politician to shame. When the kids gather for a community sing in the auditorium, the hearing impaired joined right in, "signing" through the songs.

Every Fourth of July all the children, ALL the children, participate in the Big Bay parade. Once seen, it's a sight you won't soon forget. Marble statues have been known to collect a little moisture around the eyes when those kids go by. If it doesn't affect you that way, well, I don't know who you are - and I don't think I want to.

There you have it! "Guts!" "Will!" "Sisu!" It can come in large measure in some pretty small packages - every year. And every year they have a Birthday Party - at Bay Cliff Health Camp - at the place where dreams come true - they really do.

Ω

Come On Along

Cabin Fever

There's been an awful lot of snow in upper Michigan this year. The temperatures have fallen through the basement a few times but they have managed to bounce back so the average is just a little below normal. Folks who move the snow off the roads have been too busy to do much but get tired. For the rest of us this time of year is a steady diet of white and ice and cold. When it begins to wear a little thin we call it "Cabin Fever."

Traveling to and from our cabin in the woods I try to stop by the 550 Store just north of Marquette, its Lucy's place, along the Big Bay road. I pick up a soda pop or something to chew on and always spend a few minutes passing the time with Lucy. She's a widow lady running her own business and this year the winter's been dragging her down a bit. There's so much snow the plow piles are beginning to crowd her doorway. If you're out that way, stop by and cheer her up a bit. Have a can of pop and talk a while.

Trenary, a little town thirty miles or so south of Marquette, has initiated an "Outhouse Race" festival as a sort of break-up-the-winter thing. No one from the Indy 500 has called them and they haven't heard from the NASCAR circuit but that hasn't discouraged them. My stepson, Matt, is studying at the Lake Superior State College in the Soo. He intends to be a mechanical engineer. He and a friend entered the Trenary race with a unique design of their own. I guess it could be called a design? It had all the aerodynamics and aesthetic appeal of an old refrigerator carton - that had fallen off a truck - and been run-over - several times - by BIG trucks. When I bragged to people that that entry had been built by "my step-son, the engineer," some seemed sympathetic, others just looked sidewise at me and hurried their children away. Matt and his partner won third place in the event. It must have been the sympathy vote.

While in Trenary Dorothy and I stopped by "The Hub," a little restaurant on US-41, for a bite of lunch. Dirk Wilson and his wife, Darlene, run the place. When we had seated ourselves at one of the tables Dirk looked us over a bit and from his seat at the counter and queried, "Ya wanna cuppa coffee?"

"I think I'd like hot tea," replied Dorothy.

"At's not what I ast ya."

Startled she replied, "We - aah - came for lunch?"

Dirk resignedly got up, pulled a pad from his hip pocket, and he walked over to our table. He stood looking down, pencil poised, "OK! Surprise me." That comes from too much snow and too much cold for too long. We call it "Cabin Fever."

If you happen to stop by the Hub, it's right on US-41, on a day when John Hongisto stops in just sit back and listen. John and Dirk will quickly get into a political discussion and soon you can't tell who is for or against what. I believe if one came out for mother-love the other would be against it. Dirk's wife, Darlene, just listens and smiles. She's heard it all before. Fortunately I was smart enough to take a quick lesson from her. Just sit and smile - at both of them. Don't take sides. In fact, don't say anything. The foods pretty good so stop if you happen to be hungry. Just don't say anything political.

I guess we've got to look on the bright side. Think positive. And, Lucy, when you see that big snow bank in front of your store, just think of the problem you'd have if the stuff didn't melt. Hang tough! In another week the sun will cross the equator northbound. It's called the "Vernal Equinox." It'll be up here for six months, three moving north and three moving south, and it'll cross into the southern hemisphere again.

During its visit everything comes alive again. It's a miracle, really, a resurrection! And we get to see it close up. Everything that's been cold and dead and still turns into beautiful flowers and green forests, lawns and green leaves. Animals will be out and around. Their young will be everywhere. Geese, ducks, songbirds will arrive. If you close your eyes you can almost hear that distant chattering and gabbling of a long "V" of undulating northbound geese. Even Dirk at The Hub might smile once in a while. Hold onto that memory for the next couple weeks and it'll come true.

Every experience in life is sharpened by contrast. If you've never been hungry you'll never really enjoy eating. If there were no winter you wouldn't enjoy spring and summer nearly so much. And fall! Well now, that's in a class all by itself. Aren't you glad you don't live in Hawaii? - Where everything is always the same? - all the time? Yehhk!

When you get your spirits up stop by the 550 Store and see Lucy. If you really get a high goin', stop by the Hub. Keep the faith. Under all that snow are flowers and green living things just waiting to pop out and brighten your day.

♎

Little Dog Lost

Gary and Paula Thibault of downstate Oscoda were in the Upper Peninsula of Michigan, around the Big Bay area over the July Fourth holidays. Their two teen-age children - and Renee accompanied them. Renee is their dog, a three-year-old golden retriever mix.

The Thibaults have a cabin on the Little Garlic River and had come north to enjoy a holiday away from their plastics business in Oscoda. They all went up to "Fire on the Bay," the fireworks demonstration on the shoreline at Big Bay the evening of July first. They were looking forward to an evening of enjoyment, family fun. With darkness came the main event of the evening, the fireworks display. Everybody was ready and watching. Then the fireworks went off - and so did Renee. She left the area at high speed complete with her 15-foot leash.

Renee holds a special place in the Thibault family. They've had her since she was a pup. She's affectionate, smart, and "special," especially to Paula. "The children are teenagers now," Paula explained. "They're more on their own. It left a hole in my life." Renee had eased right into that vacancy.

Their search began immediately, of course. Up one street and down another calling, "Renee! Renee!" Basically a shy dog, Renee had evidently been intent on nothing other than putting maximum distance between her and those things that went "boom" in the night.

The search for Renee followed a familiar pattern. Notices were posted: "Lost, dog, etc. etc. answers to the name Renee. Please call XXXXXX."

Time was running out. The Thibaults business in Oscoda had to be tended. They had to leave. The notices were further enhanced with color pictures. The notice coverage area was increased from Big Bay to Skanee to Marquette clear down to Rapid River. The Thibaults listed their Oscoda phone number and offered a $250 reward.

Phone calls came in. Paula followed up on every call - all the way from Oscoda to Marquette, Negaunee, Big Bay, wherever a lead took her. She always had to return to Oscoda disappointed.

One day a couple was shopping at a grocery store. The guy looks at the bulletin board while his wife goes through the checkout. He notices the lost-dog poster, the picture. On their way home they notice a dog sitting beside the road.

"Hey! That dog! That's the dog on the . . ." He turns the car around. The dog runs away. They go back to the store to get the phone number. "Hello? Say, I think we saw your dog. Yeah, with a leash. It was by the road at . . ." Paula was on the road again.

The Thibaults had received about thirty calls. Paula drove back and forth. She cruised the streets and highways following up the reported sightings. She was spending more time in the Marquette Big Bay area than she was in Oscoda. The sightings all sounded sincere. The description and details seemed valid – and Paula was determined.

Caron Christopherson of the Marquette Humane Society was sympathetic and helpful. Renee and any other animal would find a friendly welcome at the Humane Society. An advertisement, "Lost Dog," was run in the Mining Journal. The person who took the advertisement offered to join Paula in her search. Days turned to weeks turned to a month - and more. Paula kept searching, advertising, following up phone calls. No luck!

Sunday evening, the twentieth of August, Chris Kostelanski and Gary Cook were looking over some property by the Yellow Dog River. It was a remote area up near the Bushy Creek. It was getting dark. The two men thought they heard a dog barking. What was a dog doing away out here? In spite of approaching darkness they chose to investigate. They found a dog - attached to a leash. The leash was tangled in the brush.

Recalling seeing the posters around Big Bay they softly called, "Renee?" The dog seemed to respond. Could this possibly be that missing dog everyone was talking about?

Chris and Gary freed the leash and brought the dog out of the woods with them. They called Oscoda. "Say, we were out in the woods this evening and . . ."

Paula arrived the next day. The dog was Renee. Their next stop was a veterinarian. No one knows how long Renee may have been tangled in those bushes but she had lost about 20 pounds. Her rib cage looked like a xylophone. The diagnosis was nothing more than hunger and dehydration. She needed food and tender loving care. Other than that, Renee was all right.

Renee is now home in Oscoda. Gary and Chris are back in the woods.

When told of this incident, I called Oscoda and spoke to Paula. Renee is doing fine. "Paula, you sure did a lot of searching for your dog, from July first to August twentieth."

"This dog is special," she responded. "She's part of our family and we're all glad to have her home. Tell everybody 'Thank you.' All those people have been so good."

♎

Sportsmen and Women

The skills of hunting and fishing date back earlier than recorded time. It was once a necessity for survival. Hunters and fishermen and women hearken back to those early days in defense of their rights today.

We all seem to have a primal urge to venture out, to commune with nature, to obtain food for the table in the manner of our forefathers. Many rely on commercial enterprises to deliver meat to their plate. We have learned economies of scale, specialization, and efficiencies in delivering fish, fur, and fowl to the dinner plate and clothing rack - efficiencies to the point of extinction for some species.

Sportsmen and women find themselves crowded by the exigencies of time and distance. The "sport" is further away. Occupational pressures demanded their presence. Recreation has to be accomplished during a much smaller "window of opportunity." These restraints and the restrictions of private property have encouraged hiring guides. Competition has led to baiting. A customer now flies in, is taken to a site, kills something, and flies out in the morning. It all happens over a weekend. I think the "sport" has lost something.

Ω

Come On Along

The Bear Hunter

John Thompson, a part owner of the Corner Store in Big Bay, was one of the lucky bear hunters in the year's Michigan "Hunter's Lottery." John had established a bait site on August 10 and tended it regularly. He was feeding bear in the woods west of town. During the period prior to his license date he baited and watched and waited. He was able to identify six individual bear that came to his bait pile regularly. John picked two possible candidates, bear that he would "settle for" come opening day.

Opening day, Sunday, September 15, dawned blustery, cold, raining, and overcast. Undaunted John arrived early at his bait site, before dawn. He settled into his blind, and waited - and waited – and waited some more. Nothing happened. So much for his luck on opening day. The bear were probably holed up somewhere and being more sensible than John.

Monday the weather wasn't much better. Maybe it would have helped if, instead of sitting in that blind all day yesterday, he had gone to church instead? Oh well, maybe those bear will be hungrier today. Once more John came early and stayed late. Time dragged on - and on. Just at last light he detected some movement by the bait pile. It was big! It was black! It was coming to his bait pile! It was one of the two bears he had selected.

What luck! John was getting excited just telling me about it.

"It was a 60 yard shot," he said, looking me right in the eye. John raised his arms in a hunter's characteristic pose. "I raised my Winchester .270, eased the stock to my cheek as I squinted through the light gathering 3 x 9 Bushnell Scope. I held my breath - steadied the cross hairs just behind the shoulder - and squeeeezed the trigger. The recoil,' John lurched back a foot or so demonstrating the recoil, "sent a 140 grain hand loaded slug through its chest cavity. That bear ran - -"

"Sixty yards? That was no '60 yards!' Where were you shooting from? Where was the bear?" This sudden outburst had come from John's "Corner Store" partner, Pete Hall. "That distance's not more than . ."

"What? What? It was too 60 yards! I was at least, lessee, the bait pile was over here and I was . . ."

"No it wasn't 'over here.' The bait pile was down by the corner of the field. And your blind was . . ."

This heated discussion is taking place outdoors at a board table on the sunny south side of the Corner Store, the "Buzzard's Roost," a hangout and gathering place for the local Philosophy Club.

Voices were raised in argumentative protest. Arms wave, fingers point vaguely indicating direction. Items are placed here and there to represent the relative position of bait pile, blind, field corner, the location of the bear, and whatever else seems pertinent.

Frank "The Troll" Csernyik (Frank is a transplant from lower Michigan. You know, "below the bridge?" "Troll?") joined the conversation with appropriate gestures. "It was just about from here to the stop sign over there" (about fifty feet).

John's head snapped back. His eyebrows rose in indignation. "What? Why it's more than that to . . ."

Well you can imagine how that went - on and on and on.

Dennis Wilcox stood nearby leaning against the box of his pickup truck looking from one to another, taking it all in. Earl Bevins, president of the local sportsman's club, walked up about then.

"Hey Earl!" I called. "Have you seen the gen-yoo-wine 'bear finder' John bought?"

"The what?"

"The bear finder! Yeah! No foolin'! John's got a genuine, no joke, no electronics or magnetism, no electricity or battery, guaranteed not to rust, crust, bust, or corrode, rip, ravel, tear, or fray at the seams bear finder."

"It works!" John broke in, diverted from the previous argument. "You just have to attach this little fish hook to your arrow. When you shoot the bear and he runs off. This," he held up a little 'beam-me-up-Scottie' looking thing with a horizontal telescoping antenna on a free swinging pivot, "antenna will point to where ever the bear is."

"Point at the bear," queried Earl?

"At the fish-hook. See this?" He held up a little piece of blue chewing gum or something on a fishhook looking thing.

"No (expletive)?"

"I'll show you. Here! Here! Take this," John handed me the 'fishhook' gadget. "You hide it somewhere - and I'll tell you where it is. Go ahead. Anywhere. I'll find it." Sincerity, thy name is John!

I surreptitiously tossed the fishhook thing in the back of Dennis Wilcox's pick up truck.

"I'll show you! I'll show you!" John went on. "See? I'll walk over here and . . " He concentrated on his receiver gadget as he walked toward the street, the antenna waving aimlessly. "You gotta walk an arc - see," he moved down the street slowly, "and the antenna will point . ." he concentrated his attention on the meandering antenna which seemed to be pointing at the Lumberjack Tavern across the street.

"Yeah! It IS pointing, John! Maybe there's somebody in the bar with a fishhook in his pocket?" A general chuckle greeted this observation.

"No! No, you guys! This works! I was out the other night and Jeff had hid a fishhook, and I made an arc, and , by golly, I found it."

We were all kind of looking at John as if he was the reverend Jim Jones and he wanted us to drink Kool-aid. It was an uphill fight.

"Well - I don't know, John. Maybe, if the thing really works, we could get bow hunters to shoot fishhook things at bear. Then the rifle hunters could take the 'beam-me-up' thing and track them down. Maybe that'd help beat this hunting-with-dogs problem we seem to have?"

I left about then. Things weren't looking too promising for John's bear hunting story or for his bear finder.

If any of you would like more information on this "genuine bear finder," head up to Big Bay. Stop at the Corner Store. Just ask for "Bwana John."

♎

Come On Along

Survival in the Winter Woods

Global Positioning Systems! Cell phones! "On Star" emergency location systems! It would seem with the advances in our technology that we citizens of the twenty-first century need never be alone. With cellular telephones the size of a TV remote control we can call anywhere in the world from anywhere in the world. Global Positioning Satellite Receivers, about the same size as the cellular telephone, can pinpoint a position anywhere in the world to within 30 feet or less. The automotive "On Star" locator system stands ready to offer assistance for breakdowns on the highway, locating lost or stolen vehicles, and, with a telephone call, unlock the door if you locked your keys inside. Life should be pretty easy. But there are exceptions. Some of us want to be alone. We don't want all those accessories.

The north woods of Michigan's Upper Peninsula is an area where a person can wander the wilderness, enjoy the seclusion, revel in solitude, and be awed by the wondrous silence of the natural world. We find it invigorating to face the challenge of the forest, to listen to the sighing of the wind, to find consolation in the murmur of a brook, to revel in reliance on ourselves. I have a friend who tries to share these pleasures, who conducts guided tours for anyone who's interested. Let me take you on one of those trips.

The forests up toward the Yellow Dog River area are away from paved roads and tall buildings. The land is very much the way it was created. When taking a "walk on the wild side" planning and preparation is insurance. With the added burden of guiding the inexperienced scouting an area in advance is prudent preparation - especially in winter. There are three or four feet of snow and temperatures below freezing. On the day in question there's a possibility of a winter storm. Taking a partner on a scouting trip is sound practice but on this day, this happened, and that came up, and, well, you know how those things go. It turned into a solo trip.

Driving to the area up side roads and parking clear of the trail is not a problem. With skis, a compass, a small emergency pack, and a pair of snowshoes - just to have that option - the truck and the trail are soon left behind.

Heading west along an old skidding trail the going is easy. No trouble for the tenderfeet here. The scenery is beautiful. A mantel of snow turns bare trees into a fantastic winter wonderland. Everything is framed in delicate white lace. The trail wanders over an undulating landscape shaped by oceans that covered the area many eons ago. Skiing is almost effortless with gentle slopes breaking the monotony of one-ski-after-the-other travel.

What happened next was totally unexpected. Whether it was a piece of ice or a wooden stub, it was enough to suddenly turn a ski sharply and quickly. There's an unexpected twist of an ankle, a loss of balance. Everyone who's wandered the winter woods on skis has experienced this. Just pull yourself up and get on with it - but there's a sharp pain. Any attempt to move is greeted by pain. Bones are grinding against one another. The leg is broken. Further skiing or snowshoeing is not an option. And that leg hurts to beat h__l!

The forest is still just as beautiful. The lace-covered branches look down on the scene. But it doesn't seem as friendly. There's no help here. There's just silent indifference. Nature is not basically cruel but it is impersonal and unforgiving. Each creature must survive alone. There's no compassion for the weak or the foolish.

The immediate response is to breath deeply. Fight the nausea and light-headedness. Lay still. Grit your teeth. Endure the hurt. The human body reacts this way when encountering sudden shock. What makes the difference is what you do next. Gather your strength, clear your head, and evaluate the situation.

A Hollywood movie hero would prop themselves up with a gun barrel, fight through savage Indians, struggle ten miles or more through the snow - uphill all the way - and save the fort against overwhelming odds. At a time like this you realize what a bunch of tripe Hollywood is. Discipline and determination are what's needed here.

What are the choices? The truck is a half or three quarters of a mile back. With a broken leg - and with a "standard-shift" truck - there's no way you can drive. And that assumes you can get to the truck. If you did get there that side road is not well traveled. It could be a long wait for someone to pass. And there's that threatening winter storm. As if to underline that thought it begins to snow. No, the truck doesn't seem a good choice - but what else is there? The main road between Marquette and Big Bay is a half or three quarters of a mile north as the crow flies. There's a little irony. You're not going to be doing any flying. What to do?

First things first. With the snowshoes you fashion a pair of splints. Tie them in place with the snowshoe straps and some line from the emergency kit. It's slow work. It's necessary to pause frequently to fight off the pain and the nausea. There are a couple Tylenol in the emergency kit that helps some. Checking the compass you notice there's an old deer trail proceeding in a somewhat northerly direction. That helps with the decision! Its north! To the highway!

Moving is slow, difficult work. Hands dig into the snow, moving crab-wise helped by one good leg. Drag the bad leg as gently as possible. Each period of struggle moves 20 - maybe 25 feet. Rest stops are frequent - and necessary. Lessee, 25 feet in about ten minutes, three quarters of a mile is – what? Move some more. Keep moving. Where was I? Yeah! There's 5,000 feet in a mile and –

oooh it hurts. Keep moving! Don't stop too long. Keep your mind occupied, calculating, fixed on the goal of getting to that highway. Lessee, it was about 1:30 PM when you left the truck. There were people who knew where you were going, and when, and how long you should be gone. When you don't show up there will be delays, time lost speculating, wondering, making phone calls. It'll be dark.

Is that your imagination or is that snow coming down harder? Three-quarters of a mile – 5,000 feet – where was I going with that? Keep moving. A rest is just that - a rest. Mustn't quit.

The deer trail is going more westerly now. North is virgin snow and it's three or more feet deep. Maybe going to the truck would have been the better idea. Maybe just stop and try to build a fire, get warm. The snow is melting, seeping through outer clothing. Perspiration is destroying the insulating property of your underwear. And there's that pain - always that pain. Cold, that ever present villain of winter, is creeping in. Move! You've come too far to quit now! It's too late for "what ifs" and "maybes" and "I should haves." The cold is beyond "my toes are chilly." This is deep down teeth-chattering curl-up-and-die cold. A fire sounds enticing. It'd be warm! No more struggle. Just curl up and wait . . for . . . Yes! The weather is worsening. That storm must be coming. If you gathered some wood - No! No! If you're going to survive there's just one-way - north! Move!

Off that old deer trail the snow is softer, deeper. By the time your hand finds a grip, your face is in the snow. It isn't working. Another decision. What to do. Take off the snowshoe-splints. Hold a snowshoe in each hand. Now your hands stay atop the snow. You're moving again, crabbing, dragging – ooh that hurts - that leg. Rest! Move another 20 feet. Lessee, three quarters of a mile, 20 feet, three quarters of 5,000 is – rest again. Keep going. North!

During the rest periods you try giving three sharp, loud whistles - a widely recognized signal for help. If anyone is out here – if – maybe - . The only response is silence. It's the disinterested, nonjudgmental silent response of the forest. Move! Keep moving.

It's strange - eerily strange. The very stillness that attracts a person now mocks them. That's part of the mystique, of the attraction. Survival! Survival gets very personal. If you want sympathy go to a church. If you want honesty come to nature.

This situation is bad. Don't lie to yourself. If you keep going there'll be an end to the pain and struggle ahead. If you stop and wait - well - there'll be an end to that too. But you won't be here to tell anyone about it. Never give up. Never! Discipline! Discipline is your salvation. Move! Move! Despair is your enemy. Never – never - never give up. There's a road - people – survival. Its to the north. Move! Go! North!

Resting atop one of the shallow ridges you notice – what? Was it there? - Really? - A movement? There WAS movement. It was visible through the trees. It's almost, what? - Four o'clock? - And it's getting dark. Your memory recalls old time comedian, Jimmy Durante, in a lost-at-sea skit. Jimmy hollers to his companion, "Land! I see land! Row for the land!" His companion says, "That's not land! That's just the horizon!" Jimmy replies, "Well, row for the horizon! It's better than nothin'." But there was a movement - you saw movement - a car - a truck – something, probably passing on the road. "Row for the road – it's better than nothin'." The road!

Shouting won't help. People don't drive with their windows open in this weather. You're going to have to get close enough to be seen. Go! Claw with the snowshoes. Push with that good leg. Twenty feet at a time. Your spirits are higher now. The road is there! You're gonna to make it! You're gonna make it! It's – lessee - how many rest stops? Move!

You're in the ditch now beside the road. Another car is passing! You wave and shout! Nothing! They didn't see you. Twenty feet more, dragging that pain filled leg. Now you're atop the snow bank. Wait! Another car will be along.

Mark DePetro and a friend are heading for Marquette in Mark's pickup truck. Suddenly they see a figure sitting on a snow bank waving with both hands. Surprised they've gone by before they can stop. They back up and roll down their window.

"Are you goin' to Marquette?"

"Yeah," Mark replies.

"I think I've broken my leg. Could you drop me off at the hospital emergency room?"

Now that's a line any Hollywood hero or heroine would be proud of. The next move would be to save the fort and fight off the Indians.

Things were, as they say, downhill from there. Sue's leg was placed in a cast and healed well. She's grateful to Mark DePetro and is now planning - her - - next - what? Oh! Didn't I mention? That tour guide you sat in for was a young lady, Sue Belanger. Sue does an assortment of things to support her ability to live in her north woods. She's very versatile, capable, not easily discouraged, and she's my friend.

If you're ever in Upper Michigan, in the Marquette/Big Bay area, arrange a tour of our wilderness. Get 'hold of Sue. You'll enjoy yourself - and you won't have to worry about being left in the woods.

♎

Deer

We looked at each other, that little buck and I. He tried
to get me to move. I wouldn't. He finally wandered off.

Opening Day

The first day of deer hunting season in
northern Michigan begins crisp and cold and clear.
A belly full of pancakes, bacon and coffee give a
person that comfortable contented feeling. It'll also
provide fuel for warmth and the physical effort
ahead.

The eastern horizon has barely begun to get
light. Familiarity with the woods along the path I
intend to follow is going to be a definite plus. With
as little light as now exists I'll be lucky not to walk

into a tree. My objective is a "lunch camp" site under an old hemlock tree at the base of a rocky mountain. It overlooks a small valley of scattered oak trees. My thoughts wander toward the possibility of a trophy buck passing that way just as the new day dawns. There's a seat there that I had made during a previous visit utilizing the hemlock tree as a backrest. I also arranged a small rock fire pit for warming toes or toasting a lunch sandwich or for just watching the fire. I won't be building a fire just now - maybe later in the day.

The morning air is crisp and clean and clear. A few stars are still shining. On a morning like this it feels good just to be alive. I had dressed warm in case of a long period of sitting so I move slow and easy to avoid perspiring. Nothing chills a person more than working up a sweat and then sitting down for a while.

Frosted fall leaves crunch beneath my feet. The lazy days of summer are gone. Naked branches are outlined reaching toward the heavens, silent and still, resigned to the coming snow and cold. It's all part of the cycle of life in the forest.

I've started early enough that there's no need to hurry. Deer are normally a nocturnal creature, out from early evening 'til morning's light. But this time of year, during the fall rut, all bets are off. They're a lot like you and I used to be on a Saturday night. All the ladies are beautiful and you go where the action is.

The morning is dawning so beautifully I'm tempted to pause often and long just to watch the world emerge in the growing light. Aah but I'd better not watch too long if I want to be on-site when that trophy buck gets there. There'll be plenty of opportunity to watch once I'm seated under that hemlock tree.

Arriving I check to be sure I'll have clear lines of sight toward possible game locations. You have to be careful about that. It's the deer that live here after all. Changing things in their woods is like someone moving your favorite chair in your living room. You notice immediately and are wary of what's going on. You have to balance your line-of-sight clearing against tipping off the deer. If you doubt that, you're mistaken.

I don't know how long I sat quietly watching the sky lighten. The sun was just easing over the horizon and I was beginning to think prime-hunting time had passed. It was strange but it didn't really seem to matter. All sorts of thoughts came to mind. Long ago hunts in this same area drifted through my thoughts. One time I got lost just behind this hill. I was hunting with my father from our cabin, the same cabin we're using now. What got me out was a lantern showing in the cabin window. It was beginning to grow dark and, when I saw that light, I came down off that mountain like a small avalanche. Dad didn't say much but I could tell he'd been worried. I must have been about fourteen at the time.

Another memory that has stayed with me down through the years was of a successful hunt. I should qualify that label "successful." I shot a deer but had to chase it a mile and a half or so to finish it. That wounded deer cured me of taking snap-shots I didn't feel I had a high probability of killing. I feel as badly now, writing about it, as I did back then. I've only shot one more deer since then and my heart wasn't in it. I don't care to see any creature - - - There's a deer! A young fork horn buck is coming up the same ridge I had walked along. It's walking slowly, just as I had.

I've read outdoor magazine articles where a hunter spots an approaching "trophy buck" a mile or more away. This "Super Hunter" watches and predicts the animal's approach. He mentally calculates distances and windage. The ballistics of a 180-grain slug from his Bentley model 007 "guaranteed not to rust, crust, bust, or corrode" gas ejected limited edition automatic firearm have been memorized. The eight-power lens-coated telescopic sight is adjusted accordingly. Then, with a textbook shot analyzed and arranged, he waits for the deer to reach the proscribed location – which it does, of course. He carefully plans the trajectory to place the slug between the third and fourth rib so slug fragmentation won't spoil the meat. One shot and the deer drops dead on the spot. Yeah! Sure!

I don't usually see the deer 'til it darn near trips over me. I look up and there it comes. That's the way it happened this morning. The young buck approaches to within 20 or 30 feet of me. It stops and stares directly at me. I had been sitting against the hemlock, my rifle was resting upright between my knees, and I didn't move. I didn't even shift my eyes. We just looked at one another for a minute or so. Suddenly the deer shifted its head to the left, then back to the right, still looking at me. It snorted, pawed the ground, all the while watching me for any sign of movement. I didn't move. The deer didn't think I was supposed to be there but it wasn't sure. When it got no response it finally accepted the situation and ignored me. It wandered down the side of that shallow valley scratching among the oak leaves for an acorn or two. I just watched. It must have taken five or ten minutes for it to slowly work its way up the valley and out of sight behind a rock outcrop. I stared after it then slowly shifted my aching backside. That part of my anatomy had been begging me to at least wiggle a little. I looked down at my rifle and wondered, "Why am I carrying this?" The forest was silent, no answer there. The sun now tinged the topmost branches in a golden haze. I hadn't killed a deer. I hadn't even fired a shot but I felt I had had a most successful hunting experience and the world is truly a beautiful place.

Lessee now, the cabin is about a half or three-quarters of a mile back down that ridge, the same ridge the deer came up. I wonder if the coffee's still hot?

♎

Come On Along

The Woodsman

**Far from the everyday rush to instant gratification are free
running waterfalls, quiet contemplative pools, places to
". . .restoreth my soul."**

The Woodsman

Age may have slowed his pace a step or two.
The years might have worn down physical reflexes
but wisdom and experience more than compensate.
A lifetime spent in the great outdoors has given him
what most of us refer to as "exceptional woods
lore." To him that's just the way it is. It's as
normal as the sun coming up each day.

World War II interrupted his adventuring.
The United States Army sent him on another
adventure in Southeast Asia, the China-Burma-India
Theater. It was a jungle, it was hot, and it was a

whole lot different than Michigan's Upper Peninsula. When it was over he came back home.

He still knows where the wild game goes - and when - and why. He knows where the deep quiet pools are and where the hungry trout are lurking. He can take you to the rapids and the waterfalls where the action is. He can lead you beside a quiet beaver pond where marsh life lazily basks in the sunshine.

And there are campsites where ashes of bygone cooking fires kindle memories recalling tales of days gone by. It's an autobiography readable only by him. The pages he's read to me make fascinating listening.

There's a spot beside a stream where a rusted old frying pan hangs on a tree. It's been there – who knows – longer than he can remember. Passing fishermen or travelers in the outback could avail themselves of this utensil. There weren't as many fishermen back then but there were a lot more fish. Some of these sojourners might even wet a line in the creek and fry their catch immediately. The pan would then be sand-scrubbed clean and returned to its hook awaiting the next wanderer.

This was life before technological shrinkage of time and distance promoted an insatiable desire for instant gratification. Instant gratification! In the outdoors that's a contradiction in terms. In the outdoors it's the time spent on the hunt and the stream that are the gratification. We seem to have lost sight of that.

We continue to need the quiet, the solitude, an opportunity to commune with that "me" that resides deep inside each of us. Without this we become a part of the whirring machinery, the flickering electronics, and the snarl of traffic. We are no longer somebody, we have become something. And psychiatrists have developed as a profession trying to tell us this.

He's a holdover from those earlier days, my friend is. He's quiet, unassuming, and quick to offer help. There aren't many like him left. He roamed these hills and valleys when all that was here was hills and valleys. An Indian would nod sagely and say, "He knows where the center of the earth is."

Ω

Come On Along

To Order Books

Additional copies of this book may be obtained from:

Ben Mukkala
Still Waters Publishing
257 Lakewood Lane
Marquette, MI 49855-9508
www.benmukkala.com
bmukk@chartermi.net
(906) 249 9831
toll free (866) 236 1972

"Come On Along: $14.95
Shipping & Handling charge   4.05
Total cost $19.00

Other books by Ben Mukkala:

"Tour Guide Big Bay & Huron Mountains" $ 10.50
Shipping & handling   2.50
Total cost $ 13.00

"Copper,Timber,Iron and Heart $ 15.95
Shipping and Handling   3.05
Total Cost $ 19.00

Come On Along

Author's Biography

Ben Mukkala is a native of Marquette, Michigan, a graduate of Gravaraet High School in Marquette and Ball State University in Indiana. He enlisted in the United States Air Force as a Private during the Korean War, rose through the ranks, served a tour in Southeast Asia flying F-4 "Phantom" fighter-bombers. He retired in 1970 with the rank of Major.

Subsequent to retirement, he flew various aircraft, sailed boats, and traveled extensively. He enjoys the outdoors and an active life. He began writing during his Air Force career and has been published in several flying and outdoor magazines and newspapers. Marquette's Mining Journal has published his writing regularly.

He is the father of three daughters and one son, and stepfather to two sons and four daughters. He currently lives with his wife, Dorothy, in Marquette.

Ω

"Excellent and very entertaining essays written by the master outdoorsman himself."
Jerry Harju – Author – "Northern..." series

"...articles are written about hunting and fishing, family and friends and animals in his usual enjoyable style. I'm sure his many fans hope Ben Mukkala will continue to write for many years to come."
Andrew Grgurich, Marquette Mining Journal

"This is Ben Mukkala. If you want to feel warm and happy, read it."
Fred Rydholm – Author – "Superior Heartland"

"... you can almost feel the heat of the campfire coals ... fascinating narratives."
Ray Walsh, Lansing State Journal

Geofuels

Our energy use and its consequences (including climate change) motivate
some of the most contentious and complex public debates of our time.
Although these issues are often cast in terms of renewable versus
nonrenewable energy, in reality both depend on finite Earth resources.
The evolution of the Earth itself therefore offers a uniquely illuminating
perspective from which to evaluate alternative pathways toward energy and
environmental sustainability. *Geofuels: Energy and the Earth* systematically
develops this perspective using informal, nontechnical language laced with
humor. It is well suited to a broad readership, ranging from beginning
university students to lifelong learners who are interested in how the Earth's
past will influence their own future. It also provides simplified explanations
of controversial topics, such as energy return on energy investment, peak
oil, and fracking. The focus throughout is on building a sound physical
understanding of how natural resources constrain our use of energy.

Alan R. Carroll is a geologist with more than thirty years of experience
in academic research and the energy industry. He is currently a professor
at the University of Wisconsin–Madison, where he conducts research on
sedimentary basins, and he is internationally known for his contributions
to the geology of ancient lakes and the tectonic evolution of western China.
He also teaches a popular energy resources course. He is a founding member
of the Wisconsin Energy Institute and a member of the Nelson Institute
for Environmental Studies, where he is a part of the Energy Analysis and
Policy faculty. Carroll has worked as an exploration geologist for Sohio
Petroleum and as a petroleum geochemist for the Exxon Production Research
Company, and he continues to maintain active contact with the petroleum
industry through his consulting company, Geofuels LLC. He is a Fellow of
the Geological Society of America, a past associate editor of the *American
Association of Petroleum Geologists Bulletin*, and a member of the American
Geophysical Union and International Association for Limnogeology. He is
also an avid pilot who enjoys cross-country air racing in an award-winning
experimental airplane that he built himself.